Summer Snow

Summer Snow

*Reflections from a Black Daughter
of the South*

Trudier Harris

Beacon Press

Boston

Beacon Press
25 Beacon Street
Boston, Massachusetts 02108-2892
www.beacon.org

Beacon Press books
are published under the auspices of
the Unitarian Universalist Association of Congregations.

07 06 05 04 03 8 7 6 5 4 3 2 1

This book is printed on acid-free paper that meets the
uncoated paper ANSI/NISO specifications for permanence
as revised in 1992.

Text design by Dean Bornstein
Composition by Wilsted &C Taylor Publishing Services

Library of Congress Cataloging-in-Publication Data

Harris-Lopez, Trudier.
  Summer snow : reflections from a Black daughter of the South / Trudier
Harris.
    p. cm.
  1. Harris-Lopez, Trudier—Childhood and youth. 2. African American
women—Alabama—Biography. 3. African Americans—Alabama—Biography. 4. African Americans—Alabama—Social life and customs—20th
century. 5. Country life—Alabama. 6. Alabama—Social life and customs
—20th century. I. Title.

E185.97.H365 A3 2003
976.1′84—dc21
                                                              2002151024

B
HARRIS-
LOPEZ ·
TRUDIER
H

Remembering

Momma,

Unareed Burton Moore Harris
(26 April 1914 – 8 January 2001)

and

Daddy,

Terrell Harris, Sr.
(23 March 1885 – 4 September 1954)

Contents

Preface

I WAS BORN black and female in February 1948 in the southern part of the United States, specifically Alabama, which means that I was born into a sharply segregated environment in which the lines between black and white were visible and invisible, physical and mental. It means that I grew up among people who understood precisely the boundaries in their world and observed them almost unconsciously. At that time in Tuscaloosa, Alabama, there were black neighborhoods and white neighborhoods, sometimes within a few hundred feet of each other, in patterns duplicated many times over throughout the town. There were black schools and white schools, and it was not unusual for black children to walk or ride buses through white neighborhoods on their way to black schools. White businesses usually hired black workers, for few blacks owned businesses that could sustain the black community or cater to white clientele. The traditional exceptions in black business, of course, were beauty and barber shops; fish fry, chitlin, and barbecue joints (often in private homes); and funeral homes. The general pattern was that black people left their communities and went into white businesses or homes, or white-supervised jobs such as construction work, to earn their livings.

Blacks in that era knew instinctively what they could and could not do in Tuscaloosa. We could shop in a white-owned business, such as a clothing store or a shoe store, but we could not be leisurely in trying on the merchandise. Consequently, many of us grew up with ill-fitting shoes that left cosmetic scars or had more serious consequences in the way we walked. We could get credit at a white-owned grocery store, but we could not think of being cashiers there. We could walk through white neighborhoods, but we were ill-advised to linger; black women who went into such communities looking for domestic work might just as easily have dogs sicced on them as jobs offered. We could take care of white children, but we could not take our own to work with us, thus black communities mastered the extended family phenomenon in which everybody looked out for everybody else's children.

As youngsters, my siblings and I learned early to take care of ourselves when our mother had to work, to walk gingerly in the presence of whites, and to try to be as invisible as possible when we left the boundary of our black neighborhood and entered the dangerous world beyond. Or even when we entered "white" territory *within* our community. All of us routinely stopped at a white-owned grocery store a couple of blocks from home as we walked to school every day. Once when one of my older brothers asked for change for a dollar and forgot to say the obligatory "Please," one of the white owners paused, stared at him, asked him if he meant to say "Please," and generally created a tense situation until my brother conceded. An invisible boundary had been crossed despite our teachings, and the boundary had to be restored.

My world was one in which there was no such thing as trusting white people or the system of justice that controlled our lives. We were too aware of the times in which miscarriages of justice prevailed, including an instance in which my father, who owned a very successful eighty-acre farm, had been jailed for a year for ostensibly stealing a bale of cotton. It was no wonder, then, that when one of my brothers, long after my father's death, got into a fight with a group of white boys, wounded one, and ran home, my mother and her brothers were insistent that he be driven out of town, to relatives "in the country." We had no expectation that the legal system would in any way treat him fairly.

This was a world in which black adolescent girls were readily hired to baby-sit for white women and were driven to and from those jobs by the children's mother or father. When a white male was the escort — with you sitting in the back seat, of course—there was always the real or imagined threat of sexual violation. After all, we lived in a world where white men who presumed to despise blackness nonetheless fathered countless numbers of our peers. When I was once driven from a babysitting job late at night by the children's father, that was foremost on my mind. The man, whose name I don't even remember, surprised me by being perfectly gentlemanly. This was clearly an instance in which a black person in that community, namely me, was just as susceptible to stereotypes as we blacks believed whites to be.

Tuscaloosa, as I was growing up, was a town in which there was little class division among black people, or what was there was easily diminished by the fact that we were all forced to live in close proximity to one another. The teachers of black children on welfare, therefore, could easily reside next door to them or a few houses away. No matter their class, the teachers were uniformly concerned about our progress and consistently committed to keeping our parents informed about our behavior and our academic progress. It was the kind of educational system in which teachers could indeed minister corporal punishment to children—without sanction from parents or a watchful social services agency. The hard discipline of vigilant parents and teachers who expected high performance led many of the poor children who grew up with me to become very successful educators, physicians, law enforcement personnel, and other professionals.

That environment, with all its complicated transracial interactions—along with my family, teachers, neighbors, church members, and friends—shaped me into what I am today and has accordingly inspired the production of this book. The essays included here reveal some of my Tuscaloosa experiences as well as some of the paths I took after leaving Tuscaloosa. I moved from family and my undergraduate studies at Stillman College in Tuscaloosa to graduate from The Ohio State University and into academia as a professor of literature and folklore. I held my first appointment at the College of William and Mary in Williamsburg, Virginia, and from there moved to the University of North Carolina at Chapel Hill, where I taught for fourteen years before a three-year stint as Augustus Baldwin Longstreet Professor of American Literature at Emory University. In 1996 I returned to the position of J. Carlyle Sitterson Professor of English at the University of North Carolina at Chapel Hill.

These recollections and reflections are in no way designed to suggest completeness in my life or expansiveness in coverage in my formative years. Rather, they are *selectively* chosen representations of a life in black formed by intersections with various Southern forces both inside and outside the black communities in which I grew up. Some of the narratives focus exclusively on African American environments as shaping influences in my life, such as my experiences in a small black Baptist church. Other essays reflect the interactions between blacks and whites. Still others, although they do not include white people, nonetheless show the influence of whites on African American Southern people and culture. Some essays lift me out of black communities and place me in predominantly white environments. Overall, the essays illustrate how black and white my world was in Alabama and the extent to which it has remained black and Southern.

I offer these essays as indications of *specificity* within *generality*. Although I am certainly not arrogant enough to believe that my life is unique beyond compare, I have enjoyed some distinctive experiences. It is where my experiences intersect with others to evoke the "Ah, yes, I've been there" kind of response, or "I know what you mean," or "I know how you feel," however, that led me to put these thoughts on paper.

Several of the pieces included here owe their inspiration to my mother, Unareed Burton Moore Harris. Her overall philosophy of being in the world, especially as she practiced it after my father's death, has influenced her nine children and the three generations of almost a hundred persons following my parents. Her fishing and snake-killing exploits have served as fuel for storytelling in my family for decades. Her sense of honesty and morality looks over my shoulder every day. Everything I do, everything I am, I owe in large part to Miss Unareed's way of raising her children and encouraging them to be successful in a world that was not particularly concerned about their success. She was and remains my greatest earthly inspiration.

CHAPTER ONE

My Mother's Creation

I LOVE MY FIRST NAME. Black folks too generally love my first name. Although many have difficulties pronouncing it, they usually applaud the creativity that spawned it. They recognize it as being in the tradition of African American naming patterns. Black folks are inspired by Muslim-derived African names, such as Akim, Falani, and Makiba, which means that pregnant women routinely seek out name books or call public reference librarians for assistance with this process. We occasionally name our children after famous people in African American or American history (Booker T. Washington Jones, George Washington Carver Brown, John Fitzgerald Kennedy Thompson); only the name of Martin Luther King, Jr., until very recently, has remained sacred in this process. For twins we insist on same-syllable, similar-sounding names (Tiffany and Tavara, who are my nieces; Earl and Pearl; Tameron and Cameron); we would never name twins John and Alvin or Tracy and Stephen. More than anything else, we like to make up our names. So after pronunciation comes curiosity about how I acquired my name. Because my mother made it up, each time I explain, I am honoring her. Black people generally appreciate what she did.

Professionally, however, I do not operate in an all-black world. And several of the white folks I have met have had a tendency to reduce my name to the diminutive, and that's when I really have to retain my patience in telling the story. For example, I am politely introduced to someone at a lecture or a dinner party as *Trudier* (three syllables—*Tru dee uh*) Harris, and he—usually he—politely turns to his spouse and says something to the effect of "Honey, I'd like you to meet *Trudy* Harris." "Tru-di-er," I correct, always slightly surprised at how consistently white males do not listen to other people and how forcefully—and convincingly—they pass on their errors to other people. I offer the correction, and he repeats the incorrect pronunciation of my name.

It's the story of my life, brought home vividly to me recently when a white man just refused to accept the fact that there are three syllables in my first name. And he and his brothers proceeded in their hearing impairment to insist that the world be shaped as they perceive it. After all, they routinely reduce William to Bill, Robert to Bob, and that strangest change of all, John to Jack. The desire for the diminutive—or at least for a transformation of reality—seems to be in their blood.

Then—after I finally win the war of pronunciation (*if* I am able to do so)—I have to deal with the blatant curiosity. It is striking that transracial voyeurism, even this lightweight version, can exist at the level of names, but it does. More often than not, this is where the wife takes over. "Black people have such interesting names," she quips. "How did you get yours?" "My mother made it up," I counter. "Oh, that is so nice. Black people are *so* creative about names." Or, these days, "*African Americans* are so creative with names. I just love that in your culture. White people are never so creative." Now, would they seriously consider turning from naming their daughters Mary Elizabeth to naming them Ayishah Fateema or Yoruba LaQuisha? About the closest I have seen a white Southerner come to this pattern is the recent movement toward Ashleys, Laurens, and Tamekas that has crossed over into Southern European American culture.

So, in response to the curiosity, I fall into the role of potential entertainer, that position in which white people are most comfortable with black folks. If they can't control your name, they at least expect you to tell them the story of how it came to be. And I do that, but each time I do it, I call this act "fighting for my mother" because I relish any opportunity to celebrate her creativity—no matter the setting. I enjoy passing on the determination with which my mother made sure that my name was spelled as she intended it to be. Thus, the story.

I am the sixth of nine children born to Unareed Burton Moore Harris and Terrell Harris, Sr., farmers in Greene County, Alabama. By the time I arrived, five good solid names had already been dispensed. First came my three older sisters—Fannie Mae, Hazel Gray, and Eva Lee. Then my two older brothers—Terrell, Jr., and Willie Frank (who became Muslim in the early 1980s and changed his name to Husain A. Alim, which means that he probably has an even more complicated name story to tell). After my arrival, Peter, Eddie Lee, and Annie (Anna) Louise (yet another story) showed up. We were all delivered by midwives. Apparently, as my mother tells the story, she had allowed other people to name each of her first three daughters, and she decided that if her sixth pregnancy indeed yielded a girl (there was no scientific way to detect those things in 1947), then she would name the child herself.

I understand that sometime during her pregnancy, my mother went to a concert at Stillman College (later to be my

alma mater) in Tuscaloosa, Alabama. That has always fascinated me—not that she went to a concert, but that she went
to one more than thirty-five miles away from home, and that
she probably went by wagon. Anyway, that's the way the
story goes. The person giving the concert, she says, was
someone named Cordelia—she couldn't remember the last
name. She said she liked the last part of the first name
("delia"), but she wasn't particularly fond of the first part
("Cor"). Thank goodness. And in keeping with Southern
black patterns of pronunciation, she lost the "l" after the "e,"
so she heard this part of the name as "deia." With the back
end of the name in place, she still needed a front end, so she
came up with "Tru" and went for the *look* of the sound
("dier" instead of "deia") more than accuracy of original
spelling on the second part (she could do that—she's my
mother). The result was a name that had—when I first remember seeing it written—beautiful letters and a weird
sound. She called me Tru-DI-er, with the second syllable receiving strongest emphasis.

By the time I was able to assign a pronunciation to the
name, I labeled myself TRU-di-er (*I* can play around with my
mother's creation), and that's how I have been known since
—except for so many varieties of pronunciation upon first
meetings that it's been dizzying over the years. And even with
this wonderful convolution of a name, my family also assigned me a nickname—as we did for just about everybody
in the family. Most didn't stick; mine did. My younger sister
consistently calls me by that name (thought I was going to reveal it, eh?), and I would feel strange if she didn't. Of course,
there are teasing occasions when she uses the three-syllabled
name, or when she introduces me to someone, and that's also
acceptable, but it has a ring of formality for both of us. It was

with the intent of getting the family away from the nickname that when I was in graduate school at The Ohio State University in Columbus, everybody made an effort to call me by my given name. That failed, so my family has the privilege of shortening my given name to two syllables; few other people have been so allowed.

It was also in graduate school that I began to suspect that, given the potential for record-keeping in rural, farming Alabama in 1948, there was a slight chance that my name had not been recorded correctly. I did not at that point pursue the matter, however. Home for a visit in the mid-1970s, when I was teaching at the College of William and Mary in Williamsburg, Virginia, I made a special trip to the Bureau of Vital Statistics in Montgomery, Alabama, to get a copy of my birth certificate. And what a pleasant surprise that was. In February 1948 the midwife had indeed entered my name as "Trudy" Harris. However, soon thereafter, someone had corrected the spelling to "Trudier." I like to believe that my mother did that, that she liked this special creation of hers enough to want it entered accurately for posterity. She could later live with calling me "Trudy," but she knew exactly what she wanted in the beginning. It's that spirit of determination, exhibited by a cotton farmer's wife who had to quit school in the tenth grade in the 1930s, for which I fight.

I figure on being a TRU-di-er into the outer ranges of middle age, then I anticipate becoming a Tru-DI-er again. My mother would like that.

CHAPTER TWO

Three Centuries

MY IMMEDIATE, nuclear family spans three centuries, from the nineteenth to the twenty-first century. I know that might seem mind-boggling at first, but it is nonetheless true. My father, Terrell Harris, Sr., was born in Alabama on March 23, 1885; he died on September 4, 1954. My mother, Unareed Burton Moore Harris, was born on April 26, 1914; she died on January 8, 2001. My father was twenty-nine years older than my mother (yes, twenty-nine). I can only imagine how that considerably senior man must have felt capturing the heart of a tall, statuesque, golden-brown Amazon who had taken care of her ailing parents for years and would continue to do so until their deaths. He was probably fascinated as well by the sexiness of this leggy, big, brown country girl who had the good sense to be single when he met her. When they were married, it was the fourth time for my father and the second time for my mother. From their union there were born seven children (my two oldest sisters were the product of my mother's first marriage—to Jesse Moore, whose alcoholism led her to leave him and return with her two small children to the home of her parents).

I don't know if my mother knew any of my father's other

wives; they were certainly all dead or had disappeared by the time we children of Terrell and Unareed became conscious of our part in this history. However, my mother and her children were aware of one of my father's children from a previous marriage (it is unclear how many there actually were). This son, named Robert, fascinated me when I was growing up. He was this invisible brother, old enough to be my father or grandfather, who had disappeared from Alabama at some point before our father met my mother and who has not returned to this day. If he is alive, he is a *very old* man; if he is dead, he might have left any number of nieces and nephews or grandnieces and grandnephews whom I may never have an opportunity to encounter.

My father took my mother off to an eighty-acre cotton farm in Greene County, Alabama, which is where they were living when I popped into the world. As I said, I am the sixth in a family of nine. I am in the middle of my four brothers, so I like to think that my mother was especially happy to get one girl in five tries. But my mother might simply have been exhausted from having babies by the time I came along. If she were, she recovered quickly and loved us all. In fact, loving and caring for her children was my mother's primary objective in life. That became clearer decades later when her mental deterioration began—in part, I believe, because her children didn't need her to cook, clean, mend, wash, iron, and garden for them.

She had plenty of that to do on the farm, for it was one of those nearly self-sufficient operations. We had horses, cows, hogs, and chickens, and we grew the vegetables we used year-round, including corn, peas (purple hull and crowder), green beans, butter beans, tomatoes, potatoes (white and sweet), onions, hot peppers, cucumbers, okra, and watermelons. I have vivid memories of hog killings, at which my uncle Dexter, my mother's brother, presided as "the knife man." As soon as the hogs were shot or knocked in the head, hung upside down and scalded, my uncle and other men went to work scraping the hair from them. Then Uncle Dexter stepped in to do his knife art. He would make one long incision—the length of the carcass—so that the entrails could be removed. Then he proceeded with the delicate cutting and slicing that reduced whole hogs to the valued pieces that would be salted for winter eating.

Momma and other women would clean the chitlins, cut and oven-brown the skin into cracklings or eating skins, and prepare the shoulders for grinding into sausage and the head for boiling down and making souse. It was always a special Christmas morning treat to have freshly ground, highly seasoned sausage, newly made biscuits, and cane syrup (made from sugar cane instead of the less desirable sorghum).

As children in the family got old enough to help with some of the tasks, they were encouraged and allowed to do so. My brother Husain (then called Frank) had the task of feeding the neat little strips of shoulder meat into the sausage grinder one year when Terrell, my oldest brother, was doing the grinding. Frank held on to a strip of meat a second or two too long and two of his fingers followed the meat into the grinder. Luckily, Terrell reversed the blades before the tips of the fingers were completely severed. Then there was the drama of getting him to a doctor (no small feat in the country) and getting the nearly severed fingers reattached. Thank goodness the mission was successful. The only physical reminder of that incident is a slight enlargement in the tips of two of Frank's fingers.

Fruits and vegetables were just as abundant as pork in our

world. We canned enough vegetables at the end of summer to last through the winter, a practice that my mother continued long after we moved from the farm. I remember wagonloads of watermelons that my father would drive up to the back porch of our house. He would hit a watermelon with his fist, thereby busting it open, pull out the heart, give it to one of his children, and toss the rest into the hog pen. He would repeat the watermelon-busting procedure for each of his children.

My father was also a skilled craftsman. He bottomed chairs with fine strips of interlacing cane. He would sit crisscrossing strips around the bottom of a chair until they formed a nice comfortable receptacle for anyone's derriere. He was bottoming chairs one day when he heard me, following Frank's lead, cursing out the chickens. I was probably around five at the time and had no idea what I was saying (in these matters Frank, though only a year older, was considerably more mature), but my father obviously did. He whipped both of us with one of those neat little cane strips. It is the only time I remember my father spanking me. Usually he played the role of supporter and encourager. When I was picking (or picking at picking) cotton by his side one day, a big green cotton worm got on my hand. I screamed until I saw Daddy point and say, "See, he gone. He over there on that other plant." That calm voice overshadows any memory of him punishing me.

An asthmatic, my father was always seeking out new doctors to try to ease his problems. When he died in 1954 of a heart attack, it seemed only logical to connect his demise with something related to his breathing. We don't know. No one was with him when he died. He had left the house that morning on his way "to town" and had directed my mother to have the children "put the wagon in the shade." He walked down to the main road, which was quite some distance from our house, to catch a ride with someone driving by, which was apparently another regular occurrence. Standing there, waiting for his ride, he collapsed and died. My mother was told that he had a heart attack, though of course no autopsy was performed.

I remember his death as an instance in which my father got precisely what he wanted. Daddy, Momma always told us, did not want to have his children around him when he died (it seems reasonable that he would have thought of preceding Momma in death because he was so much older). He did not want to hear us screaming and crying and lamenting his departure. I believe he concluded that he could complete his Christian duty and die in peace if he were by himself; that peace would be destroyed if we were around him. As a deacon in the church, he felt it was important to labor as long and hard as he could in God's vineyard, and then to move on into eternity.

The peace he may have experienced, however, did not extend to his family. Even at his funeral—at which the only thing I really remember is being lifted up to view his body in the casket—relatives of his joined my mother's relatives in pressuring Momma to separate her seven younger children and allow some of us to be raised by other folks. She refused. I will always love her for that. Though it made our lives financially difficult, even turning us into welfare children for years, my mother kept us together. Through low-paying jobs as a domestic worker, to slightly better-paying jobs as an elementary school cook and janitor, she added her meager earnings to the slightly less meager amounts we received from welfare and kept us going as best she could. We bought groceries on credit, harvested produce from our "town" garden, and welcomed the charity of lots of people and agencies. Most important, though, we stayed together.

The older of my siblings had attended country schools in Alabama before my father's death and we moved into the "big city" of Tuscaloosa. Once Momma settled the sale of our farm (we were convinced later that she got ripped off) and moved us into town, we began attending the local all-black elementary school. The city was a traumatically different experience for us, particularly in school. We had grown up to that point on buttermilk, sometimes with corn bread crumbled up in it. To be forced to switch to "sweet milk," that vitamin D variety routinely served to school children, made us puke (literally). As "charity" children who received free lunches, we could not substitute the chocolate milk that might have been a bit more palatable.

We survived our new school environment because we were smart kids. Our teachers celebrated us for that even though we may have been "country." Gradually, except for the stigma of being welfare children, we became just as accustomed to our environment as the town kids around us. Some of us maintained honor roll grades throughout elementary school and high school. Several of us were also athletes. My brothers played baseball and basketball (Momma wouldn't let them play football), and I played softball and basketball. Not a single one of my four sisters has any interest or ability in athletics. I credit my interest in sports to being born in between my four brothers. They were my closest playmates, so I did what they did—rough and tumble sandlot football, climbing trees and hills, crawling under houses, and a host of other injury-producing activities.

My best friend during this period was Joe Ruthie. Though

we were the same age, she was much more experienced than I. Both her parents were alcoholics; she was therefore left on her own a lot to explore the world. When she told me (we were ten or so) that she had seen a man give birth to a baby, I believed it wholeheartedly. She swore by every method we used to swear that she had seen the baby pop "out of his thing." I didn't reflect on how she had managed to witness such a miraculous event; I just believed it. I was amazed that my best friend was privy to such powerful truths as this flaw in nature. She also told me that when you got married, you and your intended spouse had to perform the sex act in front of the preacher—during the ceremony. That clinched it for me. I was *never* going to get married and be so publicly exposed. Of all the juicy tidbits Joe Ruthie shared, this one was the best. It stayed with me for years. Though I lost touch with her when her family moved from our neighborhood, I often think of her. Here was a child who, with proper nurturing, could have become a great writer of fiction. In those days, however, we were happy to share secrets and get into devilment. We would crawl under the house with my brothers and bang on the exposed water pipes or join them in exploring "the ditch" behind our house. This ministream, about fifteen feet wide and eight feet deep, had enticing blackberry vines along its edges. We would climb up and down the crevices of the ditch, oblivious to poison ivy or other potential dangers. During and after heavy rains the ditch became a dangerous swirl of jaggedly rushing water. We stayed out of it at those times, but we still lurked along its shores.

If we aggravated Momma just enough, she would resort to using her one allowable curse word. "Uh shit," she would say, then, "Y'all done made me cuss." Momma never cursed because she *wanted* to. No, we little devils made her do it. Interestingly, however, her "uh shits" could emerge when we were obviously *not* immediately responsible. A dropped glass could evoke an "uh shit," followed immediately by "Uh oh." Boundary overstepped and boundary restored. A slip of the knife when cutting chicken or peeling peaches could also evoke "uh shit" and the restorative "Uh oh." Momma was good at self-censorship when it came to profanity. She had to contain herself as best she could, because she didn't want to ruin her reputation as a Sunday school teacher.

The house I remember most during this time is the one we lived in at 2513 Fosters Ferry Road. There were three rooms and a kitchen (probably no more than nine hundred or so square feet total space), a porch, and a small bathroom off the kitchen that did not have a tub or shower and that frequently had frozen pipes or an unflushable toilet. Thus we were forced to use the outhouse that was still in the backyard from an earlier era. All three rooms had to serve as bedrooms, and two of them were combination bedroom/living room/family room spaces. Our landlord—a six-foot, 350-pound, gum-chewing high yaller black man who became well-to-do by renting houses to people like us—probably felt that he was being sympathetic to this young widow and her many children by simply letting us live in this tiny space. So he did not paint it, or caulk it, or complete any general improvements. He did supply buckets of paint when my brothers and I decided to paint one Christmas. And, to his credit, in later years he added on a living room off the porch so that us girls, he said, would have a space in which to court. That one act of largesse, however, did not substantially improve the general condition of the house. We were never warm enough from the two woodstoves that served to heat two of the bedrooms (the third was unheated).

In summer snakes crawled through the crevices in our walls, and we might just as easily find a small one lounging in a bedroom corner as in one of the cracks along the porch. Taking a decent bath was impossible in any season. That arduous process began with a "number two" or "number three" aluminum tub into which hot water would be poured and cooled to a tolerable temperature. The larger of these tubs was about three feet in diameter and approximately eighteen inches high, which meant that no human being over two feet tall could ever sit comfortably in it. The tub had to be placed in an out-of-the way place, because splashing was sure to occur; location raised issues of heat in the winter. There was also the problem of sharing bath water. Two or three children could get a bath in the same tub before the water became too tepid and too dirty for further use. No matter how funky this may sound, we were still cleaner than we were before the actual process began. These "full" baths, however, only occurred on weekends. During the week we used the wash pan to clean essential parts every morning before we went to school, and we used the "foot tub," a smaller version of the larger tub, to wash our feet before going to bed on summer evenings when we had played in the dirt all day.

It was in this rust-red tar-papered house that my mother killed Santa Claus. I was twelve at the time. I was anxiously waiting on Christmas Eve with my younger sisters and brothers to see what Santa Claus would bring me. Perhaps we were staying up much longer than my mother anticipated, so it became more difficult for her to perform her secret mission. Or perhaps she was tired and needed to get her own rest. Whatever the immediate impetus, when I began speculating about possible gifts, she said, "Now, you old enough to know there ain't no Santa Claus. Go on to bed." That hurt. It hurt for many years. That year I received nothing memorable and certainly no toy. My younger sister received a doll, but I don't recall what, if anything, my younger brothers received. I do know that my mother had borne a tremendous burden trying to play Santa Claus to seven kids who had been under the age of thirteen when my father died (the youngest was just thirteen months old). She was finally forced to give it up. As for me, I became a romantic realist—always looking for Santa Claus but always prepared for him not keeping his appointment.

In other years the arrival of the Goodwill truck at our front door on Christmas Eve signaled to any neighbor who was not already aware of it that we were now charity children whom the state and other agencies supported in the little luxuries. We were the recipients of white children's slightly used toys, of government milk and cheese, and of other undesirable or unwanted items to which we dared not register objection. And most of the time my mother did not want to do so. She was eternally grateful for the help she received with her children.

The one fault I remember my mother having during this era is the one she shared with many women of her generation: she gave undue preference to masculinity. She favored her male children, especially her oldest son, Terrell, who was, by most people's standard of measurement, the model child. An A student and hard worker, whose income from jobs he held in high school helped to supplement the family finances, Terrell did not curry favor or do anything that caused Momma to prefer him and his brothers. It was simply in the nature of things. Women were put on the earth to serve men in some capacity, even if it were no more than filling their plates first at a Sunday dinner gathering. There were clear divisions between male and female work, and men were not expected to do the things, like cook, that women were intended to do. When her daughters married and brought their husbands to her house, Momma always doted on them.

When Terrell was called to the ministry in the early 1970s, my mother's chest almost burst with pride. We were all pleased with this turn of events in his life, but Momma was ecstatic. She baked lemon supreme cakes for him every time he came to Tuscaloosa from Huntsville. I never saw her disappointed or upset with him, and there was, as far as I could see, no reason for her to be. Through no fault of his own, he just managed to be the recipient of infinite motherly largesse. That was less the case with my second brother, the one who tended toward delinquency, but it was certainly the case with the two younger brothers. Once when my youngest brother Eddie and I were going out to a movie, and I declared that I was properly dressed in casual pants, my mother insisted that I put on clothes that would make me more presentable in going out with my brother.

After one of her marriages ended in separation and the other in the death of her spouse, my mother decided that she would never get married again. She would not have any male, she asserted, possibly mistreating her children. In later years, when all her children were grown and we teased her about dating, she insisted that she was not going to date and let some man take her money. "But Momma," we said, "you don't have any money." "That don' make no difference," she said, "I ain' studyin' 'bout no man." She did "study about" some man in my adolescent and teenage years, when she dated occasionally at first and had one steady relationship for several years. She could not be intimate with this man in our cramped quarters, so I guess they took care of that part of their relationship when she went to his house. He was a nice man, but he got a great deal from his romantic interest in this widow with many children. My mother cooked his noonday meal *every* day, and we carried it to him. He, in turn, cooked on special occasions, like barbecuing on the Fourth of July. I don't know why my mother eventually broke up with him, but she did, and she swore off men from that point on.

It was also in the house on Fosters Ferry Road that my family moved into the technological age. We got our first telephone on October 10, 1963, as a result of funds Frank had sent from some of his travel-related work. The number we were assigned then went from the Fosters Ferry Road house to the Lincoln Park house at 4212 Thirtieth Place, in which my mother lived for twenty-five years. It is still the number in "Momma's house," which is where my sister Ann lives today. On Christmas Eve 1965 one of the women for whom Momma worked as a domestic gave us a television set. It was quite an occasion for celebration. This television enabled my brothers and me to grow up on NBA basketball with Wilt Chamberlain and Bill Russell—when Momma wasn't insisting that we let Ann, "the baby," watch Shirley Temple movies. This "good white woman" also passed on to us our first washing machine. Momma really liked working for her and was saddened when she died, because it meant a return to domestic work in the homes of white women who were more inclined to exploit her than to help.

In one vivid example Momma related how she washed, starched, and ironed the cute play outfits for two little white girls under six. The kids would wake up from their naps and Momma would dress them in fresh outfits. Then they would go outside, turn on the hose and douse themselves, and their mother would insist that they be changed into new outfits.

The ones they had worn for less than two hours then went back into the cycle of washing, starching, and ironing. The same thing would happen if the girls got the slightest stain or dirt mark on their outfits. Outfit changes could occur several times in a given day.

It was common for us to watch our new television while munching Momma's tea cakes, for which she was known all over the neighborhood. This almost-but-not-quite-cake was what country people learned to make when they did not have enough eggs or sugar for cake. They mixed the one or two eggs they did have with an appropriate amount of sugar, flavoring, and milk. It was then poured into the well of a mound of flour (usually in a dishpan) and kneaded until it had the consistency of biscuit dough. It was then rolled out, cut into squares, and baked. These big fat squares were not sweet enough to be cookies and were too large to pass as slices of cake. They were good holding or walking food that tasted great with buttermilk. One of our cousins became so fond of Momma's tea cakes that he repeatedly requested that she make them, even after everyone in the neighborhood could afford all the store-bought cake they wanted. He contributed greatly to her reputation as a legendary maker of tea cakes.

Throughout the years of our residence at the Fosters Ferry Road house, our porch was the gathering place for the neighborhood children. Some arrived early in the morning and stayed all day; they frequently shared dinner (our noontime meal) with us. Others came and went. At times there could be as many as twelve or fifteen of us on the porch. With our unique location we could see most of the things that went on in our neighborhood. One Sunday after church, for example, when little Danny, who was about six at the time, saw the preacher's car pull up to his family's house about a block and a half away, he shouted, "Uh uh, there Rev. Walto. I gotta go home and get some fried chicken before he eats it all up." And with that he made a mad dash down the street. Everybody cracked up because we understood immediately that Danny was responding to the age-old stereotype in black communities of the chicken-eating preacher.

Long after we were well into our teenage and college years, little kids and slightly older ones still gathered on our porch. It did not matter that we did not have much in common with them. We were friendly, and we had a great porch as well as a great porch atmosphere. So they came and enjoyed themselves. And their parents got some free babysitting in the process.

When my oldest brother, Terrell, graduated from high school in 1962, he started a new trend in the family. He went to college, to Jackson State University, on an academic/athletic scholarship. That initiated two changes in our family. First, everybody else who could manage it would go to college. Second, it taught us to eat grits. Perhaps it's surprising to think of Southerners, especially black Southerners, who are not routinely exposed to grits. We were not. Our breakfast eating habits came from our farm background, which means that we had fried chicken with rice and gravy; or ham, biscuits, and syrup; or fried fish and rice; or some other such combination as our first meal of the day. When Terrell went to Jackson State and was exposed to grits, he exported them back to our kitchen. From his first trip home from college until today, somebody in my family has grits for breakfast every day—all because my oldest brother went away to college.

In 1966 I followed my brother on the college route by attending Stillman College (in Tuscaloosa), which means that I walked to school every day instead of moving away from home or living on campus. Although I was the second of my siblings to graduate from college, I am one of four to receive college degrees and advanced or professional degrees. We range in interests from mathematics, computer science, and business on the one side to English and social work on the other. Our interests reflect those of our parents. My father, although he had only a second-grade education, had the reputation of keeping his farm records in his head. He could calculate the price of bales of cotton and yields of crops with mere glances. Apparently his memory was equally phenomenal. My mother, however, was the humanist in the family, a teller of great hunting and fishing stories, a reciter of Paul Laurence Dunbar poems, and a quoter of song lyrics and biblical passages. She was a star pitcher on her high school girls' baseball team (à la *A League of Their Own*) and may have transcended her dominant humanist trait by inspiring the love of sports in my brothers and me.

As my siblings married and had children of their own, our multiple families stretched even further into three centuries. When we celebrated my mother's eightieth birthday in 1994, there were *five* generations represented in our family. *The Tuscaloosa News,* our local newspaper, celebrated that fact with us by printing a photograph and a brief article. Those five generations consisted of my mother's nine children, her twenty-seven grandchildren, her thirty great-grandchildren, and her three great-great grandchildren. And those numbers are now substantially increased.

When I contemplate the shortness of marriages these days or the dysfunctionality in families that are not separated by divorce, I like to think that Terrell and Unareed were blessed indeed to have stretched their family across three centuries. Although this feat may not be duplicated with any one in our twenty-first-century family, it nonetheless sets us apart. Three centuries provide a magical context for thinking about the forces that move all our lives: changing times and professions, different educational patterns, class distinctions, family ties, religious transformations, and the flesh that must ultimately pay the price of being human. We moved from the farm to the city, from second graders to holders of doctoral degrees, from horses and wagons to Mercedes Benzes and Lexuses, from abundance to poverty and back to middle-classness. As my mother would say, "it's more than a notion."

CHAPTER THREE

Cotton-Pickin' Authority

AUTHENTICITY. That's the issue. How did black Southerners manage to claim it in a society that devalued
their very worth as human beings, a society that certainly did
not hear their voices on practically anything? How did they
claim voice, authority, and authenticity? There was little opportunity for them to acquire it through the larger, white society, so they usually resorted to claiming it in the realm of
and within the earshot of relatives. Some of them acquired it
through the cotton picking in which they had actually engaged as well as through the mythical history associated with
cotton planting, chopping, and picking. A history in cotton
measured the distance between working class and middle
class, elementary and high school dropouts versus folks holding advanced degrees, and mother wit versus the pollution
of book learning. Having worked in cotton is comparable to
having worked in God's vineyard; it is the preparation ground
upon which all *true* Southern black experience, from this
group's perspective, is founded.

Anyone who is the daughter or son of black parents and
grandparents born in the South in the first five decades of
the twentieth century is subjected to endless tales about the
plight those parents and grandparents suffered in comparison

to what their offspring have had to endure, which the parents generally view as a less physically difficult life. Validating their experiences usually boils down to an essential phrase that might have slight variations in its delivery: "You ain't never picked no cotton," or "You never had to pick cotton, so . . ." If that phrase does not emerge in the conversation, general references to the hardship of working in cotton will serve to illustrate the relatively "easy" life descendants have in comparison to the lives of their parents.

Cotton-pickin' authority posits, first of all, that physical labor is preferable to brain work, or at least that brain work should occupy a comfortable second place in the hierarchy. There is a certain romance surrounding the people who, each spring, would get out of bed at four o'clock in the morning, hitch up their horses and mules, and be in the fields by early light to begin the process of breaking new ground for seeds. They worked all day—literally from "can't see" to "can't see"—and were still able to appreciate their families for a short while before they retired to bed to begin the process all over again the next day. The process continued with weeding and chopping the cotton during the summer, thereby nurturing it into the produce it would yield in the fall. And of course there was the physical labor associated with picking x number of pounds of cotton in a day. When I was picking cotton in the 1960s, my mother and brothers routinely aimed for two hundred or more pounds per day. On one glorious day when I was eighteen, I managed the grand sum of one hundred fifty-eight pounds.

On those brief occasions when we children picked cotton, we were mere aberrations to the usual cotton-picking system. Older folks could pick cotton six days a week, for as long as was necessary to finish up the yield from a particular crop.

When they asserted, therefore, that "you ain't picked no cotton," it did not deny the fact that you might literally have been in the fields picking. What it denied was the consistency with which you were able to *really* pick cotton, day in and day out, as a way of life. We nitpickers were just passing through. These old heads really knew what it meant to labor physically. They therefore knew how to diminish any upstart efforts we might have made to unseat their authority by referring to our puny inability to survive in a blazing hot Southern sun for more than a day or two at a time.

Implicit in the references to physical labor were notions of strength and weakness. You were strong if you could last in the fields all day. You were weak if you had to go home at dinnertime (the noon hour) and rest or not be able to return to the fields at all. When cotton picking was no longer the primary arena of work, the standard of measurement implied by cotton picking was still there. You were strong if you could accept the challenges the society constantly put before you instead of wimping out and asserting that you couldn't do something. If we complained about how long school lasted or about being tired of doing homework when we were in elementary or high school, Momma might say, "You oughta be glad you can go to school. Why, when I lived on the farm, we could only go to school for a few weeks a year. We had to pick cotton." Or they had to plant it, or weed it, or whatever else the season required. There was no sympathy for anyone in the 1960s who complained about having to sit around on their butts and read books, work math problems, learn to spell new words, or write essays. To anyone who had picked cotton in the 1930s and 1940s, that was luxury indeed.

We elicited a similar response if we dared to complain about food: "Black-eyed peas and cornbread again? We had black-eyed peas yesterday. Why can't we have fried chicken sometime during the week instead of only on Sunday?" "You better get in there and eat that food. Starving folks around the world would be happy to get what you eating. And I woulda been too when I was growing up. When we had to go to the fields to pick cotton, many times we only had a bucket with fat meat and cornbread in it. And when I went to school, we had only a baked sweet potato to carry to eat at lunch. You don't work in the fields and you get a nice hot lunch at school, so don't sit there complaining about them black-eyed peas and cornbread." This was the voice of reason, always putting into perspective the circumstances of our lives. Momma was the authority, and we might complain, but with that cotton-pickin' authority, the complaints got nowhere.

The same was true if we dared to be less than grateful about the clothes or the shoes we wore. It also brought us back to cotton and to the general deprivation that my mother experienced as a country girl isolated on a farm in Greene County, Alabama. She would tell the story of the two dresses that she owned during her school years and how she wore one and washed the other one *every day*; the dresses lasted because the school year was so short. She would also relate to us the path that she had to take to school and how rain, slush, mud, and occasionally snow made her efforts to acquire an education even more difficult. But she kept going. She suffered nearly frozen hands and being wet for entire mornings at school because the lone woodstove in the one-room schoolhouse did not give off sufficient heat for her and the other rain- or snow-soaked children to get dry. She ate her baked sweet potato for lunch. And she prized all those inconveniences, which she didn't even recognize as such at the time, because they were a step up from picking cotton.

We, by comparison, had nothing for which a complaint was justified.

Authority derived from mastering the difficult task of cotton picking also came in handy at other times. If we wanted to go to the movies (yes, there was one black theater in Tuscaloosa when I was growing up), and Momma didn't want us to go, she would emphasize that we had our yard and the fields behind us in which to play, and all that freedom was a contrast to picking cotton, so we should be thankful for it. Why should we need further diversion when we had this?

Trying to go up against cotton-pickin' authority was comparable to a staccato call and response in which you were destined to lose. In cotton-pickin' tradition some of the scenes might go like this:

"Momma, I don't like this government milk."

"Drink it, 'cause you didn't have to pick cotton to get it."

"This gabardine material Miss Daisy gave us to make dresses is ugly."

"You gon' wear 'em anyway, 'cause you didn't have to pick cotton to pay for 'em."

"All we got to do is sit around on the porch."

"It's better than picking cotton."

"Cleaning Mr. Bland's store is too hard. I have to scrub and scrub that floor."

"It's better than picking cotton."

"This blue gym suit is too big and baggy."

"And how many pounds of cotton did you pick for it?"

It took a l-o-n-g time, but we finally learned that we could *not* win against cotton-pickin' authority. We learned that we might as well embrace it as *the* standard of measurement for work and a host of other things. It always put us in our place, and it always put perspective on poverty, economics, and personal preferences. The continuum between "then" and "now" was always designed to encourage us to see "now" as preferable, as a progression that made our lives easier, although it consistently gave the power to name that ease to the "then" generation.

No matter the ages of her children, Momma would still invoke cotton-pickin' authority when it came to giving permission. She had raised us so strictly that I had not had an alcoholic beverage by the time I was a first-year student at Stillman College. Rosa, my best friend during that year (who is still one of my best friends), was from LaGrange, Georgia. She was as uninitiated in the ways of alcohol as I was, so we made a deal. I would go with her to visit her grandmother for Christmas in 1966. We would go out to a club where I would proceed to have a few drinks and she would watch over me. We would then return to Tuscaloosa, go out to a club there, and I would watch out for her. Her end of the bargain went (mostly) according to plan. We went to a night club where I proceeded to down a few rums and Cokes. I knew I was in trouble when the stairs leading down to the lower club level, where the restrooms were located, started to look like train tracks receding in the distance. That was the beginning of an ordeal that ended with her shushing me—and not really succeeding because she was giggling so much—as we tried to sneak into her grandmother's house. The next day I walked around bent over at a ninety-degree angle for the first three or four hours.

Back in Tuscaloosa the next night, we selected our club and were getting ready to spend New Year's Eve there when my mother announced, "Y'all ain't going out tonight." Oh, the embarrassment. How could she do this to me? Rosa had held up her part of the bargain, and now Momma wouldn't budge. "This girl's folks trusted her to be at my house," she went on to say, "and y'all ain't going nowhere. Ain't no telling what might happen. Things have changed too much since those days when we lived on the farm. If you were going to the cotton fields, that would be different, but you ain't going to no night club." And she continued to elaborate on the responsibility we had for this visiting nineteen-year-old female. She knew, because of her experiences as a farmer, that the other world out there was too much for two neophytes who thought they could handle themselves against seasoned, foreign forces.

So, Rosa and I had to stay home. Neither one of us has become a big drinker. I went from rum and Coke to scotch in graduate school and to bourbon, martinis, and Mai Tais in my first few years after graduate school, but it was mainly occasional, social drinking. These days I seldom have any alcohol beyond a glass of wine if I am eating out or have house guests. Rosa simply can't drink. All she has to do is look at a glass of anything with alcohol in it, and she gets giggly. To this day I have never seen Rosa drunk. And to this day I have never been as drunk as I was on that fateful holiday evening in 1966. While I won't say that my mother's farming background prevented us from becoming lushes, it was nonetheless the stone that water could not wash away.

Cotton-pickin' authority could also be used to control familial/social behavior. One of my brothers tended toward delinquency in high school, and my mother was at times in conversation with the principal or his teachers about it. After one of those conversations, or when any of us had misbehaved, Momma would make one of those self-sacrificing speeches designed to make any miscreant feel lower than a snake's belly: "I work hard for you children. I try to raise you the best I can. I take you to Sunday school and church. I have worked my fingers to the bone for you. I picked cotton so long and hard sometimes that my fingers would be bloody from where the cotton stalks scratched them. And this is all the thanks I get. You go to school and act out. Lord, have mercy, what am I going to do with you children?" Anyone who caused a speech like that to be recited was supposed to feel miserable—and probably did. Here was this widow woman raising all these little knuckle-headed children by herself, and one of them had had the audacity to act out in public. What was the purpose of picking all that cotton and trying to improve their lots if they still acted like fools? None of us wanted to contemplate Momma's bloody fingers against the backdrop of those pounds of white cotton that she picked and then dropped into the long heavy, croaker sack that she dragged behind her. The image of the hardworking, self-sacrificing mother who injured herself for the sake of her children was not a burden that any of us wanted to ponder for long.

It was even worse if Uncle Waddell, my mother's brother who lived down the street, or Uncle Dexter, another of my mother's brothers who dropped in unexpectedly at times and distinguished himself by eating black-eyed peas and cold biscuits for breakfast, got wind of some childish misdoing. Their lectures were like aches in the ears. "You children ought to be ashamed of yourself. Here yo' momma trying to do the best she can for you. I remember the time she worked from morning to night in the fields, always thinking of y'all and trying to do the best she could for y'all. She picked cotton so y'all wouldn't have to—at least not for all yo' lives. And now you up here acting up. What good did it do to take y'all off the farm? If y'all gon' act like this, you might as well be pickin' cotton."

On the lighter side, when those same uncles gathered with my mother and other persons who *knew* the cotton-picking life, there could be easy conversation about this shared experience. Stories would be told about old so-and-so who had picked an excessive number of pounds of cotton. There were also stories of how to cheat the "weigh-in" at midmorning or at the end of the day if you happened to be working in the cotton fields of some stingy white man in Alabama. "Dell," my uncle Dexter might relate in reference to Uncle Waddell, "didn't like to pick cotton for Mister Jimmy. So he would put big rocks at the bottom of the cotton sack to make it heavier at weigh-in. Now that worked as long as Dell could pour his sack of cotton into the truck bed after weigh-in and toss the rocks aside. He never got caught. But 'member how stupid Bud was. Instead of puttin' just a couple of big rocks in his sack, he put in seven or eight. Them rocks wuz clanking so loud against them scales that everybody heard 'em. Mr. Jimmy made him take 'em out and still docked five pounds from his total weight. You really had to be slick to get past Mister Jimmy."

Although I certainly was not present during that generation's cotton picking, I do remember that one of my brothers poured a couple of buckets of water onto the cotton in his sack to make it weigh more. Most cotton pickers depended on nature to supply the water, which means that folks got to the cotton fields as early as they could to begin picking while the dew was still on the cotton. Early-morning cotton naturally weighed more, so pickers had to do whatever they could in such a limiting economic environment to make the most of their labor. Even when I picked cotton in the 1960s, the price was a mere three cents per pound. In the days during which my mother and her brothers picked cotton every day, all day, it was obviously much less. Perhaps the intensity of their remarks about these experiences were designed to punctuate the fact that so much labor was given for so little economic reward. The imaginative rewards, however, were far more expansive, for references to cotton picking were the creative ground on which stood human interaction and behavior, the measurement of a mother's love for her children, and the site for entertainment among relatives.

And so it went. It might reasonably be argued that our existence in Tuscaloosa in the 1950s and 1960s was merely the foreground to the background of the cotton farming life that we had left to move to the city. It was a touchstone, an ever-ready reference point to delineate the distinctions between then and now, between mind-numbing labor and the possibility of moving to a different level of existence. It was the measure of the difference between doing what one *had* to do to survive and learning what one *could* do if one simply studied long and hard enough. It was the distinction between having lived and gathered a wealth of knowledge from those living experiences and merely speculating on what living could be. In other words, it was the difference between experience and innocence, knowledge and initiation. For those of us not properly initiated in the cotton fields of Alabama, the voices of authority derived from cotton picking served to guide our development into creative, resourceful, hardworking human beings.

CHAPTER FOUR

Dental Charity

B EING BROUGHT UP BY—if not exactly born to—poor black parents in the South has unexpected consequences. When I was in the third grade, a group of white dentists in Tuscaloosa thought that they would help the poor colored children by donating a day of services at our elementary school. The gesture was certainly well intended, for at that time I don't believe there was a single African American dentist in Tuscaloosa (one did come sometime during my teenage years). On the appointed day, a group of these dentists showed up at Thirty-second Avenue Elementary School to take care of some of our dental problems. Their answer to every cavity was simple: pull the tooth. Four of my lower jaw teeth were pulled that day, two on each side. By the end of the day, there were countless numbers of us with cotton-packed, swollen jaws spitting bloody saliva into paper cups.

Certainly we would no longer suffer the excruciating pain of biting into a piece of candy and grabbing our jaws or being awakened at night by one of those throbbing pains that would just not go away. Our parents would no longer see us crying in pain with an ache over something about which they could do little. Certainly parents in that era pulled their children's teeth; the exceptions were those strong jaw teeth with basically good roots that just had cavities. There was really no place for the parents to loop one of those infamous strings around and pull. With these charitable extractions by the white dentists, we could now move on, after healing, with pain-free mastication—or so we thought.

None of us paused overly long to consider—and probably neither did our parents and teachers—the lingering consequences for those charitable tooth-pullings. I didn't think overly much about the holes on both lower sides of my jaws until I reached college. After all, in a community in which trips to health care practitioners averaged about one every fifteen years—unless you were *really* sick—missing jaw teeth in an otherwise healthy body did not call that much attention to themselves. It was not until I was a first-year student at Stillman College and had cavities in my front teeth that I began to realize the consequences of that earlier charitable dentistry. The African American dentist who had now arrived in town crowned my front teeth and made it clear that something would have to be done about the lower jaw teeth. Otherwise, my gums would continue to recede, and the teeth in the front and back of the empty spaces would continue to shift and lean toward the empty spaces.

Now, in addition to studying Ralph Ellison (I read *Invisible Man* my first year in college), *Cybernetics and Society: The Human Use of Human Beings,* and Machiavelli, I had to contemplate my teeth. Suddenly they took on a dimension all their own. Slowly a class/education issue began to emerge. On the one hand, if I were going to stay in Tuscaloosa and work in one of the local industries, or perhaps even teach school there, then I wouldn't have to worry much about my teeth. So many people in Tuscaloosa were missing front teeth that to worry about my missing jaw teeth would seem an overly "educated, uppity" thing to do. On the other hand, if

I were going away from home—as I planned to—into environments where people placed as much value on internal health and appearance as on the external, then I would have to deal with this issue. Education and budding class issues aside, however, I simply could not afford to pay for this dental work (a teacher had provided financial help with the crowns). Other than receiving a couple of small grants, I worked my way through college. That money went directly to tuition, so my dental problems would have to wait.

They waited through graduate school as well, and of course the situation just got worse. During the wait I developed an incredible fear of having dental work done. By the time I was able to afford to have my first bridges put in—and coax myself into a dentist's office—it was almost twenty years after the charitable dentistry episode. The last tooth on my lower left side had leaned permanently toward the empty spaces in front of it, so my dentist had to be creative in trying to convince the stubborn little fellow that it had to support its part of a bridge. One of the top teeth on the left, because it had had nothing against which to rest for all those years, had protruded downward, and the bridge had to be lowered to accommodate it. The right side was even more problematic; the last tooth had turned so much toward the front that it was chancy at best to get it to support a bridge. My dentist tried nonetheless. When the bridges, called Maryland bridges, were seated, they both fitted perfectly.

That "perfection," however, was severely tested the next week. The right bridge just popped out. No creative cementing on my dentist's part would get it to stay in. So there went almost nine hundred dollars into the trash. Fortunately, the left one did what it was supposed to do. It stayed in for seventeen years. In the meantime, though, I was back to an empty space in my right lower jaw. With the strong support on the left side, however, I judged myself to be better off than before and went on about the business of living—and eating as best I could. Of course there is no correlation between one's size and one's ability to chew comfortably, or I would have been several pounds lighter than I was.

I let the situation go, in part because I was still so afraid of dentists. The dentist who seated the Maryland bridges had such a superb chair-side manner that I actually wrote him a letter thanking him for making me feel so comfortable. When he moved away from the town in which I was living, I did not think that I would find someone else as good, so I let the matter slide—again for a few years.

It was only when I bought a new house in 1996 and a dentist solicited business through Welcome Wagon that I contemplated dealing with dentists again. And just to be sure that I would feel OK when I went in to get the work done, I first introduced myself to the dentist, interviewed him (so to speak), and tried to get a sense of his chair-side manner. He turned out to be quite acceptable. It was amazing how dentists' offices had changed over the years, especially in terms of the number of gadgets designed to soothe the savage dental patient. There were television screens above the dental chairs with soothing pictures of flowing streams and the sounds of bird life, or patients could elect to don head phones and listen to CDs (I was even encouraged to bring my own music), or patients could put on dark glasses and pretend that they were anywhere else but the dentist's office.

This dentist and I shared interests in charitable work, sports, and a host of community issues. He occasionally told (bad) golf jokes as I sat in his chair. After he thoroughly examined my teeth, he sent me to an orthodontist who began the process of preparing my right jaw to receive implants. That in itself was an interesting—though not a particularly painful—saga. At the end of it, I had two beautiful implants and a solid bite on the right side of my mouth. Just in time, too, because the left bridge decided to make its exit the year after I received my implants. Through a delicate five-tooth extension process, I now have a new bridge on the left side. So, finally, after almost forty years, I am no longer discriminating in my chewing from left to right. I have equal lower jaw chewing power.

I would imagine that the dental charity I received in third grade has cost me close to thirty thousand dollars. And that's only in dentists' offices. I can't begin to estimate what it has cost me in dental floss, toothpaste, mouthwash, and those special little brushes you use to get under bridges and implants, and between bridges, implants, and natural teeth. Nor can I begin to estimate what it has cost me in brushing and flossing *time*; if I were to value that time at twenty dollars an hour, I would be pretty rich. Most of all, the cost to me psychologically has been immense—the fear of going to dentists (until I found a couple of wonderful ones), the fear of my remaining teeth developing problems that would cause them to have to be removed, the fear of a bridge popping out during a lecture or while I was on a trip and the emergency care that would be needed (that happened to me once), and the more mundane fear that some strange odor is exuding from my mouth because too many unnatural components now reside in it.

Charity. It seems like such a wonderful idea. I wonder, however, if those dentists (and of course I don't remember any names) ever paused to think about the little colored children from whose mouths they pulled so many teeth in 1957.

Did it occur to them then or later that they had permanently changed the lives of those children? Did they ever pause to think that, because they did not elect some alternative to tooth pulling, some of those children have suffered through-out their lives? Or did they just remain smug in the notion that they had done their dental good deeds for the week, or the month, or the year? In how many other schools did they volunteer? How many other children around Tuscaloosa have suffered as I have? Did those dentists ever stop to consider that serving fewer children by filling their teeth might have been a preferable alternative to simply yanking out every child's teeth? Would they have remotely done the same with their *own* children? In a society where dentistry is so much about *saving* teeth, why did they not try to save ours? And what—beyond some implicit human caring, which our racist society obviously negated—would have obligated them to do so? Was the task just too overwhelming? When faced with so much need, did they simply do the best—as they judged it—they could and then walk away?

And what of the African American principals and teachers who acquiesced in receiving this charity? *Did* the consequences ever occur to them? Or was this another instance in which they thought that it was better to negotiate what they could and—to their minds—help some kids rather than try to opt for more extensive dental work from these dentists? Perhaps few if any of them have ever even thought about what happened that day at the Thirty-second Avenue Elementary School in Tuscaloosa. Perhaps I am the only one—or one of a few—who have linked such an extensive part of their dental history to this one life-changing moment. Perhaps.

Yet I have contemplated this event for years. I am always struck by the fact that these white dentists came to a black elementary school and *put their hands into black children's mouths.* When I read and teach Maya Angelou's *I Know Why the Caged Bird Sings* and come across the part where Maya's grandmother Henderson takes Maya, who is suffering from a *horribly* painful tooth—to a white dentist in Stamps, Arkansas, and he proclaims, "Annie, my policy is I'd rather stick my hand in a dog's mouth than in a nigger's," I always pause and contemplate the fact that those white dentists came to our elementary school. They came. They stuck their hands in our mouths. Arkansas is only a few miles away from Tuscaloosa. Although my experience was in 1957 and Maya's was about twenty years earlier, not much had changed in the South. So, on the one hand, perhaps those white dentists deserve credit, indeed thanks, for their charitable work; on the other hand, however, it is one of those gut-wrenching instances in which out-and-out prejudice might have been preferable to the consequences of their "liberal" actions.

This is a tale of segregation setting into motion a sequence of events in which the actors met and interacted without getting to know each other, but in which—at least on one side—the encounter was profoundly disturbing. It was one of those instances in which you would like to re-create a meeting of the principal parties forty years later and see what the other side has to say—*if* he remembers. It goes without saying that the circumstances would have been different if Tuscaloosa had *not* been segregated, or if black dentists had practiced there at that time, or if the white dentists who came had selected an alternative to the solution they chose. Salvaging a worthy lesson from it all is difficult, and yet the fact that I remember and reflect upon the event must ultimately have its own value. It is a striking instance in which well-intentioned people reached across racial lines and produced consequences that were more human than racial, more economic than prejudicial, more colorless than black or white. Nonetheless, when the consequences of segregation are manifested at the level of one's taste buds, the politics of racism are as constant as eating.

CHAPTER FIVE

"Would you go out with a white boy for five dollars?"

WOULD YOU GO OUT with a white boy for five dollars?" The voice came from the driver's side of the car across the passenger seat and through the open window into earshot where I was walking. Startled, I glanced over to see what I could make out of a youngish-looking white man driving a car through a black neighborhood and pausing long enough for me to respond, which I did instantaneously. "No." I was in the sixth grade. I was walking about two blocks ahead of my mother and other family members who had been to my elementary school for a PTA meeting and a time of open classrooms in which parents could meet with teachers. I was thinking back to the events from which we were just leaving, because Mrs. Bennett, the sixth-grade teacher whom I adored, had just given my mother a favorable report about my performance in her class. I had done so well that she had invited me to come to her house the following weekend to help her and her daughter prepare for a club meeting that she was hosting. That meant that Angela and I could eat all the cocktail peanuts we wanted as we dusted and rearranged chairs for the gathering. And we would have access to the little sandwiches that had been specially prepared for the party, once all the guests had been served.

My family obviously lived in a black neighborhood, and the school was about six blocks from home. Because few people had cars, no one ever gave thought to doing anything except walking that distance. We did it day and night, rain or shine, winter and summer. I never contemplated the possibility of those six blocks being violated by a "white boy" who had come from who knows where to try to buy "black gold." As a person who was not sexually initiated, I had also given little thought to what it meant to go out with any boy, let alone a "*white*" boy. The fact that he had a car, which only a few of the older people in our community had, was striking. The fact that he drove the car into our neighborhood was even more striking. And the fact that he thought he could just pass through, select a black female body, proposition it, and drive away with it to some unknown place in which he would proceed to "go out" with it was most striking of all.

"Would you go out with a white boy for five dollars?" From his perspective *who* or *what* was I? To him I was, first of all, black—or probably "Negro" at that time—so that gave him license to ask the question. I was, second of all, female, so that reduced me to a vagina. I therefore became the site for his sexual initiation and/or his sexual pleasure. I was also anonymous, which meant that he could therefore get some of the "p" word, disappear back into his community, and no one but the buddies to whom he was sure to confide the episode—*if* he had been successful—would know. Most important, to him I was sexually available, probably responsive, and undoubtedly would not be too offended if some anonymous "white boy" drove by and asked me to have sex with him. And, again, even if I had been offended, would it have mattered?

Though he ran risks approaching an anonymous black female, he did not weigh those risks sufficiently. I could have been older, taller, and bigger. Because I had chosen to walk ahead of the other black folks, and since he had driven by them on his way to me, I could have been carrying a weapon. I could have yelled, screamed, or cursed him out. I could have called for my family, and we could in turn have surrounded the car, pulled him out, and beat the crap out of him (if we had been violent types). I could have had some incurable disease, including a sexually transmitted disease. Apparently none of this weighed on that "white boy's" mind. He was clearly being driven by some urge that was stronger than reason. Was he about to get married and wanted a bit of practice before the big day? Was he about to go on a huge date, something like a prom, and wanted practice for that reason? (It was spring, so prom season was certainly near.) Was he just horny? Or was he a sexually experienced "white boy" who believed all the hype, all his society's sexual folklore, about black women, the kind that James Baldwin portrays in his short story "Going to Meet the Man"?

"Would you go out with a white boy for five dollars?" I'm guessing this white boy was a neophyte, poor and/or cheap. I label him neophyte because of the nearly pathetic, beggarly way he approached the task he had set for himself. Slowing to a halt, politely requesting, then speeding away as soon as the single-word response was uttered. He was probably on the black side of town because he was a virgin, or at least a virgin at trying to have sex with black girls. I label him poor because young white men raised in middle-class families in the South did not have to go out under cover of darkness pursuing the remote possibility of getting some anonymous black female body to have sex with them. Young white men from "good" families would have used the maid and/or her daughter for sexual initiation. It is the kind of practice that writer Raymond Andrews documents so vividly in his first novel, *Appalachee Red*. It is the kind of practice about which my mother told us stories when we were growing up. Two of her male cousins were strikingly different in skin coloring; one was high yaller and the other coal black. The lighter one, she explained, was that way because his mother had worked for Mr. So-and-So down in the country in Alabama, and he "had had his way with her." In such a situation, Momma maintained, the woman "couldn't help herself."

If the "white boy" was not poor, but he was just a skuzzball slumming in a black neighborhood, then he was decidedly cheap. Five dollars for a good sexual encounter in 1960 was not a flattering offer, or perhaps that is simply because of the eyes with which I look back on the incident. He obviously thought that amount would be acceptable to any black female body. By offering a mere five dollars, he not only labeled me as sexually available but as a prostitute as well. The financially offered exchange did not remotely encompass the possibility of call-girl status; it was to be cheap, quick sex.

He was also a neophyte because he called himself a "white *boy*," which probably meant that he was sexually uninitiated, still a virgin, and needed the cover of darkness to hide that status from himself as much as from any prospective partner —and his excursion into black territory certainly hid it from the white folks. From this perspective his trip to my neighborhood suggested that he was desperately trying to earn status as a "white *man*."

"Would you go out with a white boy for five dollars?" This

"white boy" understood his history. As with the folklore about black women, he knew what actions and spaces were available to him in the South. He knew that he could, with impunity, drive his car into a black neighborhood and possibly leave with a black female body in it. And indeed he might have found such a body that night, for I have no way of knowing how long he drove around the streets on the black side of town. He knew, as well, that if he had simply grabbed a black female body and raped it, there would be no repercussions. And even if he wanted to identify a black female who would become his concubine and then make trips to her house—even in the daytime—he knew that there would be no repercussions. It was well known in our neighborhood that the police car frequently parked during the daylight hours in front of one black woman's house meant that the white policeman driving that car had chosen her for sexual favors. Whether she liked or loved him might have been irrelevant (and I never knew the whole story). He had undisputed, unchallenged sexual access to her.

I never knew if this woman in our neighborhood also had a black male lover or husband. If she did, he clearly had no power in this historical configuration. He was silent and/or invisible. His position is not unlike that of my cousins' "father," the one who had to remain mute while Mr. So-and-So "had his way" with his wife. Once that nonblack "black" baby was born, his choices were limited. He could swallow whatever pride he had, accept the child, and raise it as his own (with the visible sign of his powerlessness constantly before his eyes). Or he could leave his wife because of this child, which would mean that the children he had actually fathered would also suffer (and leave-takings were rare in the country). Or he could respond violently (as Andrews's character does in *Appalachee Red*) by beating his frustration out on his wife. Whatever choice he made would not erase the impact of the white man's effect on his manhood, his marriage, and his family. He was caught in the same tangled racial relationships that the "white boy" I encountered brought into our neighborhood.

His presence in our neighborhood meant that the "white boy" was carrying out a history of power relationships with black people. True, his trip was about sex. But it was more about power. Sex he could have had on his side of town. But he felt free to come to our side of town, to violate spatial boundaries by going across the tracks, so to speak. In a way I could say that he had gotten "out of his place," except for the fact that white men in the South in 1960 considered their place to be wherever they drew the line.

Consider the implications of his power play. He did to us and our neighborhood what we could not do to him and his neighborhood (not that we wanted to). No young black man born in Alabama before 1980 could have conceived of driving into a white neighborhood even to pick up a white girl for a date, let alone cruise through trying to solicit a strange one for sexual favors. Besides, few white girls would have been out walking home from a school function. Their parents would have been driving them in cars. When the "white boy" made his trip into our community, he essentially screamed at us: "I can come into your neighborhood, but you can't come into mine. I can screw black women, but black men don't dare think about screwing white women. I can get away with this because of the history to which I am heir. You can't even think of duplicating it. So what if I don't score this time? That doesn't change anything. I still have the power and the history that you never will."

So far, I have envisioned this episode as fitting within male history. But what of the women in that history as well as in this "white boy's" life? Did they condone their men pursuing sexual favors from black girls and women because they considered sex, as they have sometimes been stereotypically portrayed, too nasty or inconvenient for their frail bodies? Did this particular "white boy" live with his mother? Did he have sisters? If he had sisters, were they dating age? Did he consider how men might have approached them? Did he care?

"Would you go out with a white boy for five dollars?" What if I had been what that "white boy" was looking for? What if I had been stupid enough, curious enough, daring enough, or financially needy enough to get into that car? Would I have been writing this essay today? Would I have ended up raped by the side of the road somewhere? Would I have been taken to the kinds of houses I came to hear about later, those in black neighborhoods in which savvy middle-aged black businesswomen rented rooms by the hour to those in the know? Would I have been beaten up and abandoned? Would I have simply been the partner in a business transaction that, upon conclusion, would have found me returned safely to the point from which I had been plucked? Of course those are the roads not taken, and I am confident that I am better for not having done so.

"Would you go out with a white boy for five dollars?" Although I did not take the "white boy" up on his offer, he won figuratively in the sexual contest, for he seduced me into thinking about him—unnamed and only partly known—throughout the more than forty years since that chilling encounter. Even as I write this, I recognize that he has seduced a portion of my imagination. Because I am not likely ever to cross paths with him again, I have here given him immortality. And still he fascinates me. For all my later-learned knowledge of his history and of how sexual race relations work in the South, I am still struck by the daring with which this somewhat timid sounding "white boy" made his request and disappeared. Have I occasionally haunted his imagination in the same way? Or did he just find another black female body later that evening or the next evening and notch his sexual gun with one more black conquest? Did it matter to him at all that one lone black female in Tuscaloosa said "No"? Would he have been shocked to discover that I was only in the sixth grade, and that he could have run the risk of statutory rape?

"Would you go out with a white boy for five dollars?" "No." But perhaps, finally, it doesn't matter, for I am nonetheless caught in the exploitive dynamic that allowed this "white boy" to ask his question. This dynamic is a part of the South and its history and is something most black Southerners are still trying to make peace with. Although I believe I have made my peace with the episode, and while I am pleased that I had been conditioned by my family and community to shoot back that emphatic "No," it was ultimately perhaps as effective as spitting into a whirlwind to change its course.

CHAPTER SIX

Porch-Sitting as a Creative Southern Tradition

I HAVE RECENTLY been reflecting on the significance of the porch in the South, on what that space allows and what it means. I have been thinking about the history of sharing and interaction that characterizes porch space in Southern culture, about the voices that bring the space to life, about what this space has meant historically and creatively to almost everyone in the Deep South. Before proceeding, however, a definition is in order. Throughout this discussion, the word "porch" refers to the physical attachment that protrudes from the *front* of the *first level* of many houses and business establishments in the South. I emphasize *front* and *first level* because I do not wish to identify wraparound porches, or verandas, or balconies with the activities I describe; I am concerned with those spaces that face *directly* on the street, with an unobstructed view of traffic along the road or walkway or, as came later, sidewalks. Such porches were certainly a phenomenon of the nineteenth century, but I am primarily concerned with the time period in the first five or six decades of the twentieth century, where yards might have been a solid expanse of dirt and where walkways would probably not have been paved. The porch is usually not enclosed, though it may be screened in, and it is covered by an extension from the roof of the house, with appropriate supporting joists. Frequently, house owners add swings suspended by chains from the overhead beams, accordingly called "porch swings." But rocking chairs and straight-backed chairs are the usual furniture, and of course people can sit on the porch steps.

"Porch-sitting" is an activity in which people can participate from early morning until late at night. All they have to do is plop their bodies down, engage someone in conversation, and the *activity* is on. I emphasize activity because I interpret porch-sitting to be dramatically different from "porch-staring"; a single individual can sit on a porch and stare at the world passing by, and obviously lots of people have done that. However, porch-staring lacks the interactive quality that I believe is key to porch-sitting. Keep in mind, however, that "porch-staring" can be upgraded immediately to porch-sitting when a second person joins the first one on the porch, or when that person interacts with people on other porches or with those who are passing by.

For example, when I was about twelve, I was sitting on my front porch steps early one morning, just staring—elbows on knees, legs gaped wide apart—when I heard this voice from the porch across the street, up the hill, saying "———[she used my nickname, which I will not share here], sit according to your family." That was the voice of Aun Nance Ann, and she, like every other woman in the neighborhood, had the right to chastise any child in the community. So I straightened up immediately. More recently, when I was home in Alabama on the Fourth of July and out about 7:00 A.M. doing my walking-jogging routine, I passed a porch-starer—just sitting there, watching the grass grow. He gained porch-sitting status when he yelled out at me, "Out mighty early this morning." "Yeah," I responded, "gotta keep that fat off." "You gon' cook out today?" "Naw, that's just more fat to work off." "Well, don't you get too hot out there." "I won't." Now, these are examples of porch-sitting at its most minimalist, with the briefest of interactions. The activity is obviously more appropriate in warmer months, but because the South is so temperate, there can be extended seasons of clinging to the porch.

The *activity* of porch-sitting can involve a great variety of things. Porches are where Southern women have traditionally removed at midmorning to shell their peas or make other such preparations for dinner (that meal we Southerners eat about 1:00 P.M.), to do some of their sewing or other portable work, or to visit with each other. For children, especially during the summer months, porches offer an inviting space for entertainment ranging from imaginative play to playing with toys to hiding out beneath the floor. For older non-working men, such as the one I encountered, porches might be the preferred space all day—either at their own homes or at neighborhood gathering places. They gather to play checkers, talk politics, reminisce, or discuss crops, weather, and anything else that lures their imaginations. For working men porches are where they retire after their evening bath to wait, with their families and sometimes their neighbors, for the houses to cool off sufficiently for everyone to go to bed in peace. These evening sessions can provide the most fruitful opportunities for traditional storytelling; folk characters such as Brer Rabbit and the mythical slave John make their entrances along with jokes, ghosts, and plain old gossip.

In 1982, I explored this evening phenomenon in a lecture

called "Southern Black Folklore in the Twentieth Century: Can Brer Rabbit Kill Television?" In this talk I generally lamented the fact that television, video games (remember Pac-Man?), and other more enticing forms of entertainment were supplanting the evening sessions on porches. That development, along with the advent of air-conditioning in every nook and cranny of the South, is transforming and threatening with extinction the porch-sitting tradition, especially the evening portion. Today, there are certainly signs that the tradition still exists. But it is obviously not as strong now as it was when I was growing up, and the tradition was probably not as strong then as it was for my mother and her siblings growing up in the 1920s and 1930s. This change and potential loss is all the more reason to consider what this activity is and what it offers participants.

The location of the porch is crucial. It is that (some critics would say) liminal area between private (inside the house) and public (the street) space. It is the natural squatting space for people you might like well enough but wouldn't particularly want in your house. And because notions of Southern hospitality would not allow for turning them away, you can always invite them to sit on the porch. It is the space where housedresses or bathrobes can be worn with impunity; if a person so dressed were to step into the street, neighbors would probably raise their eyebrows. It is the space where the person sitting can control what is going on in the house even though he or she is not physically inside the house; in other words it's good hollering space, as when a mother calls out, "Joann, check the water in them beans!" or "John, you done made up that bed yet?"

More important, perhaps, than the glimpse—figurative or

literal—inside the house is the view the porch provides on the world. That window allows for observing anything and everything that comes into view. Let me give you some examples. I spent my formative years in Tuscaloosa, Alabama, at 2513 Fosters Ferry Road. That house, now no longer in existence, was at the bend of a dirt road with a full view of the other houses. (Imagine a boomerang with my house at the outer curve.) That formation gave my family, especially my brothers and sisters and me, a great view of what was happening "up the road" toward town or "down the road" toward the country. Periodically, there would be a car chase through our neighborhood, which usually meant that the police were chasing a black man who thought his car could outrun theirs. I remember witnessing several such chases from our porch. It was like walking into a theater in the middle of a drama. You could observe the sword fight that was going on, but you had no idea what had caused it or how it would end. That five minutes' worth of drama could stimulate porch conversation for days.

I also remember witnessing fights between Monkey and Lida Mae. They lived down the road toward the country, but they came to Miss Gert's, the bootlegger's house, two doors away to get their daily shots of alcohol. Again, we were spectators to dramas that, from our perspective, began in medias res. All we knew was that Monkey and Lida Mae would occasionally come out of Miss Gert's house fighting. Remember, I said fighting, not wife-beating. They would curse and scream at each other, engage in fisticuffs, back off, curse some more, then the fisticuffs again. Neither was sober nor strong enough to inflict serious damage on the other. They simply fought. Surprisingly, the fighting never interrupted their progress toward home, so we had a steady show for three or four blocks. We watched and commented on this from the porch because that is where my mother insisted that we remain during this turmoil. What we considered—and what *was*—entertainment was the bane of this Christian neighborhood. We never thought about the implications of violence between people who presumably loved each other. We never passed judgment on the woman who sold liquor to these people who obviously could not handle it. We never thought about the vantage point from which we watched. We simply watched—from our porch window on the world—and, as Zora Neale Hurston would say, we chewed up the lives of those people with our gossipy responses to their actions.

We also watched one of my male classmates put on his mother's stockings and high-heel shoes, dresses, and makeup and parade up and down the street. Although we all considered it unusual, we never considered it abnormal. And nobody registered any objections. It was just another of the watching events available to us from our porch window. Unlike the police car chases or the drunken fights, where participants did not care one way or another about our watching, my classmate paraded up and down the street precisely because he wanted an audience; we could call out to and interact with him, and he could do the same with us. He turned our window on the world into his public stage. And we, who were busily watching were in turn being watched and evaluated by the performer for our assessments of his performance. Mirror on mirror—it was an interesting dynamic.

Looking in. Looking out. Offering comments either way. The porch was and is a two-way mirror. It is easy to combine the viewing with work. I remember those occasions on which we had bushels of corn to shuck or peas to shell in midsummer for immediate eating as well as for freezing or canning for the winter's food supply. In August it would be peaches—seemingly tons and tons of peaches—that would be frozen, canned, or, if we were lucky, layered with sugar in a crock jar to become peach brandy in the winter months. The women would shuck, shell, peel, and talk. Fingers or knives moved as fast as the conversation, and children big enough to be helpers could learn a lot about people and activities in the neighborhood.

It was here that I learned of the impending marriage of a couple of my neighbors. Getting married was routine; what made this one interesting was that she was *older* than he. Buzz. Buzz. We watched from our porch as they came home after the wedding—to the house across the street and up the hill from us (the same one in which Aun Nance Ann resided). And it was announced throughout the neighborhood that they had fried chicken, rice, and gravy for their first meal in that house. Porch-sitters, I'd like to think, were perhaps the original grapevine.

Quilting always elevated porch-sitting a notch or two. People passing by were always curious about the quilt. And it was quite a feat to get those quilting horses positioned just right if the porch was small. Fingers and stitches vied with tongues as tales were related about who wore what. I think of the vividness with which folklorist and filmmaker William Ferris captures that tradition in two of his films, *Two Black Churches* and *Made in Mississippi: Black Folk Art and Crafts.* And I think of the quilting venture that Mama Day and her sister Abigail engage in as they sit sewing on Abigail's porch in novelist Gloria Naylor's *Mama Day* (1988), making a double-ringed wedding quilt for Cocoa and George. Family history and personality inform their sewing as engagingly as they informed the sewing traditions on our porches in Tuscaloosa. Black women created art out of the pieces of fabric as they created art out of words. The porch became their "word-shop" as assuredly as novelist Paule Marshall's kitchen served the same function for the Bajan women among whom she grew up.

Children could claim porch-sitting as their own activity anytime the women did not need the porch for something they were undertaking. Playing in the swing, challenging its endurance. Rocking away in the rocking chair. Performing for adults in the evening. My nieces and I, on those occasions when I vacationed with my older sister in the country, would on a rare evening stand in front of the porch and sing for the adults seated there. "Will the circle be unbroken? By and by, Lord, by and by." "That sounds good," my uncle Dexter would say. More frequently, if there was trouble to be gotten into on the porch in Tuscaloosa, we would find it. But we also had to pay the consequences on the porch, for it was there that we would be switched for all the world to see. Switching was bad enough, but we shared with large numbers of Southern children the humiliation of having to go out and find our own switches. And if we dared to get ones that adults judged too small, they simply sent us back for larger ones. Punishments that today would probably reap a gaggle of social workers screaming child abuse were routine in those days, and none of us is particularly worse for wear. After all, one of the challenges of porch-sitting was to see how much devilment you could get into before some adult caught you pulling another child's hair, pinching somebody, or taking a child's favorite toy away.

Things usually settled down in the early evening, and the

porch became an extension of the house in another way. It was here that, after running around barefooted in the dust all day, we washed our feet in an appropriately named "foot tub." This was the era, remember, when children did not bathe every night because there was no indoor bathroom with a gleaming white bathtub. This was the heat-your-own-water-and-pour-it-into-a-metal-tub-to-bathe era. Because feet were the most abused and dirtiest parts of the body, they had to be washed every night. After all, in the absence of electric washers and dryers, cleaning dirt from sheets by boiling them in a cast-iron washing pot was hard work indeed. The nightly foot washing at least cut down on a portion of that work. Thus "cleaned," we could settle down and listen to the adults take over the porch-sitting routine.

The zone that the porch occupies is the realm of creativity, with its intense interactive engagement. In storytelling sessions, whether during the day or in the evening, porch space signals license—license to exaggerate, to lie, to enter into verbal contest with family and neighbors. Porch space occupies the border between the "real" world and the world of storytelling, an invitation to audiences to put aside their daily cares and go where the storyteller takes them. The person who begins a tale thus steps onto yet another stage. Not only is he or she on stage performing the tale—verbally as well as physically, with gestures and exaggerated body movements— for the listening audience, but he or she is also being evaluated for quality of performance. A stage for subject matter and its quality of presentation. A stage for performer and his or her quality of performance.

Jokes and funny stories were favorite forms of narrative interaction on our porch, especially when my sister Hazel and her husband, John, would arrive to sit for a couple of hours with us. John liked to tell jokes, but he could barely get himself through a single one without balling up in laughter, tears streaming down his face. I think I remember those sessions so well because his laughter was as entertaining as the stories and jokes. Somehow, there always seemed to be a story floating around about bare feet or tennis shoes—you know, the plain white cloth ones (we polished them for gym class) or the high-top black ones ("buddies," we used to call them). In one tale the mythical slave John prays to God to take him to heaven because he's tired of dealing with white folks. "God" comes in the form of Old Massa in a white sheet, and John discovers that he really does not want what he prayed for. "God" insists that he come with him, however, and John "obeys" by taking off running down the road, with "God" chasing him. When John's children begin crying, their mother tells them that "God" cannot catch their father because he is barefoot. Tales abounded about black men in tennis shoes outrunning cars to escape some kind of trouble. When I later heard comedian Bill Cosby's routine on tennis shoes, it was like déjà vu. Porch-sitting in the evening allowed black folks to wrap themselves in laughter even as they were wrapped in darkness, watching fireflies buzz and keeping mosquitoes away by smoking rags in a bucket.

Porch-sitting could also be applied to courting relationships, for the swing was usually reserved for the courting daughter and her beau on Wednesday and Sunday nights. At times, other family members could join them on the porch for the usual storytelling or other interactive sessions, but more often they were left alone—under the watchful, behind-the-curtain gaze of parents, of course. Younger children, ever eager to interrupt the courting process, usually had to be driven from the scene under threat of whippings from parents or worse from the daughter. Hand-holding and polite kissing were allowable, but woe to the young man and woman who tried anything else.

Such courtships on porches have found their way into Southern literature. One of the most striking instances occurs in a scene from writer Margaret Walker's classic novel, *Jubilee*. While entertaining her beau and several other young people, the daughter of the owner of the plantation (where the heroine, Vyry Brown, is enslaved) inadvertently belches and breaks wind on the veranda after a dinner party one Sunday evening. Now that is something pedestalized Southern white ladies simply don't do. The embarrassed Southern belle escapes inside the house, but Southern gentility must be upheld. Her mother insists on some rectification and enlists the aid of one of the enslaved young black men, who is a "dumbwit," in her effort to restore the status quo. The height of the absurd occurs when, on the porch on the next courting night, the young black male stands silent before the guests and when recognized, takes claim for the previous Sunday night's offense. "Evening to yall. I come around here to take tha fart on myself what Miss Lillian farted last week."*

Porch-sitting at business establishments is endemic to Southern history as well as to Southern literature. In my home neighborhood in Tuscaloosa today, Mr. Adell owns a little grocery store comparable to the one Miss Vera owned when I was growing up. The neighborhood grocery usually stocks a few staples, but mainly it stocks things few people need but everybody likes—candy, cake, sodas, and so on.

---

* Margaret Walker, *Jubilee* (1966; reprint, Bantam, 1969), 91.

Its primary customers, therefore, are the children who shop there during weekdays, but especially before and after Sunday school and church. Its primary porch-sitters are male. They are the men who cultivate the sizable field behind the store, from which Mr. Adell supplies just about everybody who wants them with fresh collards, corn, turnips, and okra as each is in season. Or these men work elsewhere and just pause on the porch to rest. They occupy the four or five chairs available and always seem to be engaged in earnest conversation when I pass by.[*]

This 1990s manifestation is not unlike Hurston's description of one of the most famous literary porches in America. The porch in front of Jody Starks's store in the fictional Eatonville, Florida, in *Their Eyes Were Watching God* shares much with historical barbershops in that it is a talker's paradise. It is the space where reputations can be made or nipped in the bud, where talkers engage each other for the sake of entertainment or to stimulate their own argumentative imaginations. Contest is foremost, and that contest defines a male world. Two of Hurston's male characters, for example, engage in a lengthy discussion on human nature and expound on whether it is nature or caution that protects humans from danger. All the lines are familiar to the crowd gathered, but they amen good points made and egg on the contestants to outperform each other. What is ever new is the performance, and listeners judge each contestant as to who is most up to the task on a given day.

Just as men earn reputations for talking, in Hurston's world they also shape reputations for women. Budding

---

[*] Mr. Adell died after this essay was written. His store is now abandoned.

sexuality and seasoned femininity get equal applause from the men who watch the women passing by. Sometimes the women join the porch-sitters, joke with them, or playfully act out courtship rituals; other women walk by in carefully selected outfits, chosen especially to evoke the verbal applause. Consider one of Hurston's interactive exchanges.

But here come Bootsie, and Teadi and Big 'oman down the street making out they are pretty by the way they walk. They have got that fresh, new taste about them like young mustard greens in the spring, and the young men on the porch are just bound to tell them about it and buy them some treats.

"Heah come mah order right now," Charlie Jones announces and scrambles off the porch to meet them. . . . "Gal, Ah'm crazy 'bout you," Charlie goes on to the entertainment of everybody. "Ah'll do anything in the world except work for you and give you mah money."

The girls and everybody else help laugh. They know it's not courtship. It's acting-out courtship and everybody is in the play. The three girls hold the center of the stage till Daisy Blunt comes walking down the street in the moonlight.

Daisy is walking a drum tune. You can almost hear it by looking at the way she walks. She is black and she knows that white clothes look good on her, so she wears them for dress up. She's got those big black eyes with plenty shiny white in them that makes them shine like brand new money and she knows what God gave women eyelashes for, too. Her hair is not what you might call straight. It's negro hair, but it's got a kind of white flavor. . . .

"Lawd, Lawd, Lawd," that same Charlie Jones exclaims rushing over to Daisy. "It must be uh recess in heben if St. Peter is lettin' his angels out lak dis. You got three men already layin' at de point uh death 'bout yuh, and heah's uhnother fool dat's willin' tuh make time on yo' gang."*

Although most of this banter is disinterested, it can indeed become sexual. Consider Toni Morrison's "up South" version of this phenomenon in her novel *Sula*. Young teenagers Nel and Sula, on their way to Edna Finch's Mellow House for ice cream, pass by men who "drape themselves" "on sills, on stoops, on crates and broken chairs," waiting to be distracted, particularly by women.† The girls pass by precisely because they want male attention. When Ajax calls out "Pig meat," they get what they want. Their budding sexuality and potential attractiveness have been recognized by one of the most desirable men in the Bottom. It will be many years before Sula actually sleeps with Ajax, but the lingering memory of that porch acceptance probably informs her reaction to him as much as her own fully mature sexual desire.

In the most devastating verbal contest that takes place on the porch in *Their Eyes Were Watching God*, Jody and his wife Janie play the dozens about the effects of aging. Usually passive and silent when Jody shames her in front of the porch audience (made up primarily of men), this time Janie retaliates. The incident is certainly not planned, but it is no less devastating. In a space where Jody has watched reputations be bolstered, especially sexually, he must now see that his own sexual reputation is severely damaged if not destroyed. When Janie cuts a plug of tobacco unevenly, Jody uses the occasion to comment on her getting old and incompetent: "I god

---

* Hurston, *Their Eyes Were Watching God* (1937; reprint, Harper/Perennial, 1990), 63 – 64. Hurston also includes comparable scenes in *Mules and Men* (J. B. Lippincott, 1935) as well as in her autobiography, *Dust Tracks on a Road* (J. B. Lippincott, 1942).
† Toni Morrison, *Sula* (Knopf, 1974), 49.

amighty! A woman stay round uh store till she get old as Methusalem and still can't cut a little thing like a plug of tobacco! Don't stand dere rollin' yo' pop eyes at me wid yo' rump hangin' nearly to yo' knees!"*

It is a serious mistake for Jody to mix up Janie's abilities with her physical looks. Because she is considerably younger than Jody, she quickly straightens him out:

> "Naw, Ah ain't no young gal no mo' but den Ah ain't no old woman neither. Ah reckon Ah looks mah age too. But Ah'm uh woman every inch of me, and Ah know it. Dat's uh whole lot more'n *you* kin say. You big-bellies round here and put out a lot of brag, but 'tain't nothin' to it but yo' big voice. Humph! Talkin' 'bout *me* lookin' old! When you pull down yo' britches, you look lak de change uh life."†

A man of Jody's pomposity cannot take this humiliation, and it is embarrassing even for the listening audience. Nonetheless, the scene illustrates that if one elects to act out a drama on this stage of competition, then one is liable to suffer the consequences. If the porch has not been kinder to lesser men, then why should it bow to Jody just because he owns the space?

In another manifestation of this liminality, the porch in front of businesses historically was the place where blacks and whites could pass or linger with each other legitimately before the segregation of service inside the stores or the segregation of society beyond the store porch. In an interesting literary representation, author Lewis Nordan creates a store porch in *Wolf Whistle,* a novel based on the 1955 murder of fourteen-

---

* Hurston, *Their Eyes Were Watching God,* 121.
† Ibid., 122–23.

year-old Emmett Till in Money, Mississippi. Here, black people sit on the front porch of the white-owned grocery store
and white people sit inside. Blacks and whites pass each other
freely on the porch, but inside blacks are served only after all
whites have been attended to. Of interest is the fact that
blacks and whites listen to the blues music that one of the
black porch-sitters plays. It is on the porch and inside the
store (the porch's mirror image) that the shock of the Till
character's comment to a white woman is discussed briefly
and interpreted before all the black folks disappear. The porch
space itself has not represented a violation of Southern
norms, but for a young black man to speak to a Southern
white woman in a sexual way is outrageously beyond the
norm. Sexuality that can be applauded on Hurston's porch
serves as an impetus to murder when uttered from the porch
of the white business establishment.[*]

Transitions in architecture and demography have had a
profound impact on the tradition of porch-sitting. In the
ormer village environments in the South, where few people
in a community owned automobiles, or if they did, they did
not have a garage for them, people could easily amble by
each other's porches and interact freely. Then builders or
owners began to devalue traditional porches—as more and
more Southerners retreated to their air-conditioned houses
—and created instead those little overhangs that barely pro-
tect you in the rain before you can get into the house. Another architectural transition resulted in carports and garages
taking up the space once allotted to porches. A few stalwart
souls tried to move the site of porch-sitting activity from the
front and center of the house to the front and end of the

---

[*] Lewis Nordan, *Wolf Whistle* (Algonquin Books, 1993), 22–39.

house. Porch-sitters retired to their carports. That is all that remains of a porch at the new house to which my family moved in 1970. My mother used to sit there intermittently all during the day, engaging her neighbors and scores of relatives in conversation, reminiscing about growing up, and watching every bit of activity that went on in the neighborhood.

Together with these architectural transitions, Southerners discovered suburbs.* Sidewalks disappeared or were so far from the houses that few people could talk across that space. Houses were set back, sometimes by hundreds of feet. Dwellers hid themselves behind lush shrubbery and curving driveways. There was little reason to sit on a porch—if the owners had one built—because you could only engage the folks in conversation who actually made the trek to your space. An overwhelming desire for privacy supplanted interaction and openness, and that impact on the tradition of porch-sitting is still being felt.

This desire for privacy has led to the latest manifestation of the transformed porch-sitting space, that phenomenon known as "the deck." Its location, at the back of most houses, is a primary signal that its function is antithetical to the traditional porch. It exudes privacy. More frequently than not, it looks out over woods or over someone else's equally private backyard. It sports railings and can be too high off the ground to encourage uninvited entry—even if someone were to go to the back of the house. It says that the owners want to get away from everything interactive—except with the people they specially invite to share that space. The deck, in other words, is control, privacy, and lack of access writ large. It is one of the latest invasions of the South and is part of that ever

---

* I am grateful to Southerner Alex S. Jones, who was one of my fellow residents at the Rockefeller Study and Conference Center in Bellagio, Italy, in October 1994, for raising this point.

increasing standardization of American culture. Everywhere in America must look like everywhere else in America, and Southerners are slowly giving in to the deck part of the look-alike-ness.

I like to think, though—and I admit that this is pure unadulterated romanticism—that there are pockets in the South where porch-sitting has survived whole, as writer Alice Walker would say. Where during the day as well as in the evening, people can engage themselves and their neighbors in the exchanges that reflect a way of life, a relational way of being, one that ties people to their families and their neighbors as well as to passersby. Where to "sit according to your family" is as much a cultural and creative imperative as a behavioral one. Where interaction is the norm. Where "staring" might be boring, but where "sitting" is joy.

CHAPTER SEVEN

The Overweight Angel

A UN SIS WAS ONE of the angels who got misplaced. Instead of coming from the right side of the throne and descending down to the miry clay of the earth, she got coughed up from the devil's furnace and never made it more than six inches off the ground. You see, she miscalculated her historical time periods and somehow got the idea that Satan was still as angelic as the day he was booted out from up there and that she wouldn't get tainted from the association. Starting with this basic misconception, she took it upon herself to right the wrongs of the world, which to her was our tiny neighborhood in Tuscaloosa, Alabama. The community consisted of one street and perhaps thirty houses and a grocery. Not being one to admit even a potential for mistakes, Aun Sis continued on her shaky foundation until her charges in our neighborhood moved, got married and disappeared, died, or otherwise removed themselves from her influence.

She was nobody's aunt in particular. At least none of us could trace any bloodlines directly back to her side of the oven, but she delighted—sometimes to our chagrin—in claiming all of us. Not only "us," meaning the children, but our parents as well. Some of the women her age were even calling her "Aun" Sis and the title did seem to add a bit of authority—warped though it may be—to the huge woman who made it her business to tend the business of our lives. She must have been all of 250 pounds. When she stood up she was an easy six feet barefooted. You can well imagine why she succeeded in passing out so much free soul saving. She towered over everybody, including her diminutive husband, whom the neighbors fell into the habit of calling "Mr." Sis.

It was amazing how Aun Sis managed to get into so much of her neighbors' business without leaving her seat on her front porch. But she did. That was partially because she lived across the street from the grocery and any self-respecting family in that area had to make at least four trips to the store per day. So Aun Sis would sit there bombarding them with questions or drawing them onto her porch with the sheer force of her voice. If you didn't get over there fast enough, she'd let out with: "Well, there, Miss Frosty, didn't know you wuz gittin' above yo' kinfolk these days. 'Cose I 'member the time when you ain't had a pot to piss in nor a window to th'ow it out of. But since you big enough to know where fertilizer come from, I guess you don' 'preciate relatives no mo'." Believe me, it was the scum of the community for a week who would let her finish that speech.

Poor Mrs. Johnson, who couldn't hear very well, should have thanked the Lord that she couldn't at times. Aun Sis would start in on her when she was a good forty feet away from the store.

"Hear tell that boy of yourn got in trouble with the law again," Aun Sis would say. "Tried to tell that fool he ain't the President's son, but naw, he wouldn't listen. How much time he git this time, Bertha?"

Mrs. Johnson would continue making her way slowly to the entrance of the store and lean more heavily on her walking stick. She was already slightly bent and seemed to stoop even more doing that last thirty feet or so. Maybe her bending was natural because it was a known fact that Mrs. Johnson left her hearing aid home to escape the remarks she knew would be hurled from Aun Sis's porch. Or her bending might simply have been from the knowledge of entering Aun Sis's territory.

When Mrs. Johnson offered no response to Aun Sis's comment, the silence by no means stopped the assault.

"Bertha," Aun Sis would bellow, "I know you hear me talkin' to you. Been tellin' that lie to everybody for years like you can't hear, but I know better. I knew you when you could hear a gnat piss twenty feet away. So jes cut that deef mess out!"

Mrs. Johnson would wait until she got to the store and directly across from the porch, then she would look up and say, "How you, Sis?," turn abruptly, and walk into the store, not allowing Aun Sis a chance to catch her eye and respond.

As soon as she saw Mrs. Johnson coming out, Aun Sis would start again.

"When that boy of yourn git outta jail, Bertha, you brang him to Sunday school and church. Teach him to turn from the ways of the wicked. You tell him I said he oughta pray while he there in jail. Be good for his soul. And don't forgit to brang him to church."

The attack never ended until Mrs. Johnson was completely out of earshot, even if she had been able to hear.

Another way Aun Sis stayed in everybody's business was through the frequent trips her friend and relative Cut'n Coot made to her house. Cut'n Coot lived at the far south end of the street, around the one and only bend in the road, and she kept Aun Sis posted on that neck of the woods. Cut'n Coot was Aun Sis's twin in every way except height. Aun Sis also towered over her, and it was felt that she even threatened her into bringing news from around the bend. A gossip flunky, that's what Cut'n Coot was. But it didn't seem to matter very much. The voice and its echo were perfectly harmonized.

I remember once when I was fourteen and Momma sent me to take some canning jars to Aun Sis. Cut'n Coot and Aun Sis were sitting on the porch taking people apart with their lip service. Aun Sis never would cease her attacks when children were around because she felt that if they knew how grownups acted, they wouldn't grow up to be that way.

"Chile," she was saying to Cut'n Coot, "I wuz sittin' here and she come walkin' down that road right out there. Jes a switchin' her tail as drunk as you please. Musta spent the night at Bootleg Gert's."

"Lawd, naw," came the echo's reply. "You hush yo' mouf. Did she have on that little bobtail black dress again?"

"Um huh, so short you could see her tail feathers."

I tried to interrupt.

"Momma said she sent these jars for you to put your canning in."

"Jes put 'em down over there. . . . And you know, she dared to raise her voice and try to speak to me—me, a church-goin' woman. You know I don' cotton to that kind of thang."

I put the jars down and listened almost against my will. Aun Sis continued: "And she wuz draggin' that little whimperin' snotty-nosed youngun behin' her. Had on a T-shirt and nothin' else. Hollerin' to the top of his voice. 'Cose you know they say it ain't her husband. Look jes like that man what live next door to her. You know the one."

"I sho do. Umh, umh, umh. Ain't that scandalous?"

The conversation continued as I descended the steps and

started home. It was only one of many about Mrs. Taylor, our neighborhood drunk and scene thrower. And Aun Sis always fell just one short of saving Mrs. Taylor's soul by delighting so much in discussing her sins.

Aun Sis was worse than the mail service. Rain, shine, sleet, or snow she was sitting on that porch. Only a blizzard could have driven her inside, but such phenomena are unknown in that part of Alabama. When it was a mere eighteen or nineteen degrees, Aun Sis put on her light overcoat and survived off her fat. In fact, if you stepped on her porch on the coldest of days, there seemed to be a certain amount of warmth exuding from the great lady. Perhaps that was because of her origins. Anyway, she would sit there and keep up her various tirades against the neighbors.

Aun Sis continued her bullying and misdirected soul saving throughout my junior high school years, but the year I started high school was the year she met her pepper salt. It came in the form of a pint-sized runt by the name of Sary Jane Rebecca Addison (named for two grandmothers and an aunt). Sary moved into the neighborhood and transferred to the local high school. Her family occupied the house that Mrs. Johnson used to live in, thus suggesting it was destined from the beginning that she not get along with Aun Sis. Sary's mother had died six months before, so perhaps Aun Sis felt a special obligation toward Sary because she had no children of her own. But Sary didn't feel particularly like returning the obligation. This revealed itself the first time she made a trip to the now famous store across from Aun Sis. It was the beginning of spring, on a Saturday afternoon, and Aun Sis was sitting there busily trying to force a couple of flowers to grow when she saw Sary switching up the street. She had on a bikini top and a pair of short shorts. Aun Sis swiftly concluded that the devil was in our midst and that this child needed her soul saved.

" 'Roun' here," she directed to the fast-approaching Sary, "we dress accordin' to our family."

"Well, I'm sure glad my family isn't from around here," the impish Sary replied. "I don't take to sheets very well." It was obvious that Sary had been warned about Aun Sis and obvious too that Aun Sis had *not* been warned about Sary. The big woman almost rose from her seat in a show of surprise, but changed her mind halfway up. She couldn't let the devil get the upper hand. Mustn't let the child know of her startled reaction. She sank back into her chair, more determined than ever that she should save Sary from the throes of the wicked, and come Judgment Day, present her soul as a shining offering on the altar of the Lord. Thus determined, she decided to take a new approach with Sary. Instead of insults, threats, or insinuations, she would use logic.

"What I meant, Sary," she tried again, "wuz that the little boys often git the wrong ideas when girls don' cover up their bodies. Goin' 'round 'sposed like that might cause 'em to think you easy."

"Didn't cause Daddy to think that way about Momma and this was her favorite outfit."

And that's probably why you so backward, Aun Sis undoubtedly thought—no home training—but she didn't say a word. And for that woman to be speechless was in itself something miraculous. The miracle was only momentary, however.

"Didn't yo' mama teach you no respect for yo' elders?" Aun Sis asked.

"Sure she did and she told me to be especially respectful to Aun Rebecca 'cause she gets a bit trying sometime."

Unwilling to be led or pushed from her course, Aun Sis responded.

"What about strangers? Didn't she tell you to be kind to 'em? What about that?"

"My Momma," said Sary, looking directly at Aun Sis and pausing for emphasis, "told me not to talk to strangers." With that, she turned and walked into the store. The interval gave Aun Sis time to revamp her attack or her rescue, depending on your point of view. She had a long reverie, because what she didn't realize then was that Sary had a part-time job at the store on weekends. Cut'n Coot provided her with this bit of information when she joined Aun Sis on the porch. They were both there to greet Sary when she came out of the store three hours later.

"Hear tell you got a job over there," Aun Sis started in. "Mighty fine thang for younguns to learn the value of work at a early age."

"That's what my Momma always said, Miss Sis." Sary had also rejected the kinship title. "But from what I can see, some folks didn't get the proper training when they were growing up. Momma always said idle minds were the devil's playthings and there seem to be a lot of them around here."

"You wouldn't be tryin' to git sassy, would you girl?" Cut'n Coot asked. "We can take any little sassy tail in this community and whup her butt good."

"Now, now, Coot," Aun Sis cautioned. "Ain't no need to threaten the chile. She wuzn't tryin' to make it personal . . . wuz you, Sary?"

"No ma'am, Miss Sis, but Momma always said it was a good practice to apply the truth of a thing to yourself once you saw it. See y'all later, Miss Sis." Sary made a fast exit down the road and around the bend, leaving the two ladies no further along on their crusade than they had been before.

The fireworks between Aun Sis and Sary became so well established that idle spectators would try to find their way near the scene with one excuse or another whenever the two were scheduled to confront each other, which was almost every day. For almost two years the war continued with Aun Sis trying to convert, moralize, and otherwise change Sary and Sary resisting almost effortlessly. Aun Sis forgot that she had other charges in the neighborhood and concentrated all her energies on Sary. We suspected that deep down they probably liked each other because they made such an effort to disagree, insult, and otherwise maim each other.

Sary succeeded fairly well in starting a new trend in the community. All newcomers during that two-year period invariably called Aun Sis by her recently bestowed appellation —Miss Sis. Other ladies in the area were accustomed to such address, but you could see Aun Sis's displeasure whenever it was applied to her. That is, you could see it every time any of the new people used the title but not when Sary used it. Aun Sis was still very much determined that Sary would never see her upset, angry, or in any way displeased.

The final scene between the two occurred on the day of our graduation from high school. Sary refused to take off her gown after the ceremony and we soon found out why. Upon reaching home, she put down her diploma, took off her shoes and started up the street. She didn't have to work that day and could have only one destination in mind.

When she reached the spot directly across from Aun Sis's porch, she stopped. Aun Sis was sitting there as usual. She had seen Sary coming and waited in anticipation. She knew that Sary must have something to say and held her tongue to give the heathen first go.

"Hey, Miss Sis!" Sary called, as if Aun Sis might have been thirty yards instead of thirty or so feet away. The greeting was unnecessary because she already had Aun Sis's attention. Perhaps she wanted to emphasize the distance between them; she had never once set foot on Aun Sis's porch. The present arrangement had always been the normal talking space between them.

"Miss Sis," Sary addressed her again. "I just wanted you to be the first to know that I'm leaving this neighborhood. Getting out of this town. Going away forever. You're not going to have me to yell and scream at anymore. And I wanted you to know, too, that I'm going unconverted. That church stuff was too much. Doggone bunch of hypocrites. Always telling people, 'Go cleanse yourselves,' and never looking at their own morals, and their own souls. I am sick and tired of that. I am sick and tired of do-goodies trying to straighten out my morals when they're already straight. I am sick and tired of this old narrow-minded neighborhood. But mainly, *I am sick and tired of you*. That's what I came to tell you too, but that doesn't matter anymore cause I'm leaving."

Aun Sis, somewhat immune to Sary's backtalk by now, simply asked: "Where you goin', Sary?"

"Up to Knoxville to college," she answered in an "I've got something on you" kind of voice, and turned and made her departure.

Aun Sis bowed her head and smiled.

CHAPTER EIGHT

"Make a Joyful Noise"

MAKE A JOYFUL NOISE UNTO THE LORD." In the kind of democratic churches in which I grew up, injunctions such as this were easy to follow. This one means that, in church on Sunday morning, you should holler at the top of your voice—whether you have a recognized singing voice or not. People were kind and overlooked your screeching, because they never did know whether they were standing next to someone who was truly *in the spirit,* or if they were harboring the next Aretha Franklin. So some folks *sang* and everybody else hollered. We liked to think of it as being in that great African tradition in which it is believed that everyone who has a voice can sing. No Juilliard School of Music. No singing at the Met. Just folks, down home, singing for the sake of praising the Lord.

Some of my earliest exposures to making joyful noises were the songs with which the church deacons would begin each Sunday's worship. One of them would sing the first line of a song by himself, rather rapidly, then the others and the entire congregation would join in singing the same line at a tremendously slower pace. This was called lining out hymns and apparently emerged from the period in which songbooks were not readily available. A song leader would therefore "line out" the song line by line or verse by verse. "Shall I be carried to the sky on flowery beds of ease? No, there's a cross for every one, and there's a cross for me." Many of the songs so lined out were referred to as "old Dr. Watts," after one of the most famous songwriters. Indeed, the deacon who lined out the song might hold a tiny book (no more than two inches square) to which he glanced occasionally as he sang through the lines and verses.

When I was old enough to try to participate in this process, I had two problems. First, I could barely understand what the solo singer was saying; cadence and pacing were challenging to say the least. Second, the slower pace of the congregational response to the lined-out line was even more challenging. I always seemed to be a phrase or word ahead of where they were. I began to feel that this was some kind of fraternity into which I would never gain entry (and the secret-looking little book didn't help). It wouldn't do to ask somebody what people were singing when—that would be admitting that you were somehow not of the fold. I was well into my teens before I could hear and sing those songs correctly.

You could move from that mass of congregational singing on Sundays to the select groups of the various choirs. It was still a matter of singing or hollering. I liked going to church and participating in all its activities, so I joined the junior choir shortly after I was baptized at thirteen. Baptism occurred after I had graduated, so to speak, from the mourner's bench, that first pew in the front of the church to which non-members are encouraged to go during revival meetings. From Sunday through Friday night a visiting minister would preach his heart out in an effort to get young folks to come into the fold of the church. I got up from the mourner's bench on a Thursday evening in September 1961. I didn't see a great vision or encounter a Jesus who lifted burdens from my back, but I did feel as if I could live within the strictures of the church. Besides, it provided the opportunity for me to join the choir.

Let me be clear. The fact that some of us hollered was no fault of our musical director. She was a talented and devoted musician who did the best she could with the lesser talented and the far less devoted twelve-to-eighteen-year-olds over whom she presided. As far as directing goes, Mrs. Brown directed her heart out and, in that great tradition of younger choirs that grace so many African American churches, we sang our hearts out—as best as talent and immaturity would allow. We were challenged to learn new songs, and we did. And we sang them with great gusto.

Of the fifteen or so of us who made up the junior choir, I was the only participant from my family (my siblings didn't even pretend they could sing). The Cannons, however, would have five or six of their stair-step daughters singing in the choir at any given time. Polite and well mannered, these girls could at least carry a tune. Their problem, therefore, was not lack of talent. It was giggling. One or the other of them was liable to start giggling—sometimes with good reason and sometimes just for the heck of it—in the middle of a song in church on Sunday morning. If the offending one were lucky, she could get back into serious singing after a few titters. Mostly, they were lucky. Then came a fateful Sunday.

We had prepared for that Sunday by learning a new song. It was fast-paced and when learned, brought that surprise of accomplishment that follows reciting a complicated tongue-twisting rhyme four or five times in succession. The words and phrases were simple; the trick was to remember to put them in the right order. It was an old spiritual about how the newly converted feel after their transformation is completed through baptism:

> Ducked in the water
> Come up shouting
> No more doubting
> He will hear us
> And be near us
> We'll be given
> Bread from Heaven
> He will feed us
> Until we want no more

Simple enough. Unless you got the lines out of order and threw somebody off. The singing was so fast that it would be difficult to recover. Anyhow, Joan Cannon forgot some of the words and started saying things like "peas and cornbread/ taters and maters" (potatoes and tomatoes) and practically turned the choir out. Although most of us contained ourselves and kept on singing at this breakneck, breathless pace, Joan's sister April couldn't control her giggling and burst out laughing. Right in the middle of what was supposed to be an uplifting praise song. There she was, cracking up while standing up, then sitting down in the middle of the song, and continuing to laugh uncontrollably. It was, in the vernacular of the day, "a scanless." And Mrs. Cannon was indeed scandalized.

It's hard to apologize for bursting into laughter during church service, especially when you are in the middle of singing one of "the songs of Zion." Mrs. Cannon grounded April for a week and refused to let her sing in the choir for the next two months. Poor April was so tickled by it all that she could never get in the proper frame of mind to feel as if she were being punished. (But then, how does one punish someone for being, as they determine it, "disrespectful" to God? After all, couldn't laughter be considered one of the "joyful noises" that God might find pleasing?) All anybody had to do to get April laughing again for the next several weeks would be to mention those "taters and maters." I remember this episode because it was so much a part of the democracy of singing in historically black churches, at least in the small down-home environment in which I grew up.

Big cities, however, are not like down home. It was in the big city of Atlanta much later in life that I found out that *some* black Baptist churches actually had people audition for the choirs, especially gospel choirs. For us in Tuscaloosa, it had just been a matter of "y'all come and sing. Of course we will practice, but y'all just come and sing." Not so in Atlanta. My goodness, I thought, what would the angels think? How can you be required to pass a test in order to make a joyful noise to the Lord? Well, live and learn. There it was. And not only were there auditions, but in the church I attended they were judged by a single person—the minister of music—whose talents were, at best, in the B range. So how could a less than angelic warbler dare to determine who would make the joyful noises unto the Lord?

Even more striking with the Atlanta gospel choir was that the music was not original. If it had been, that might have provided some *slight* justification for the need for wonderful voices to bring it to life. But the music was all imitation. Kirk Franklin and other gospel greats provided the inspiration of the day. It was thus a matter of trying to duplicate those radio or CD voices—every Sunday morning, in practically every African American Baptist church in Atlanta. Churches whose choirs most closely approximated the recorded sounds were generally the ones that received the most applause.

Discrimination against certain singing voices within these kinds of African American churches seems the height of incongruity in terms of religious practice. Are we singing to make a joyful noise to the Lord, or are we singing for the sake of performance, for the "form, fashion, and outside show to the world"? Are we being hypocrites in the very institution in which we are supposed to be most altruistic and egalitarian? Do we believe that it makes a difference to God if someone sings off-key? Is He going to assign places in Heaven based on whose singing voice is best, who brought out the largest audiences, or whose *performance* was most applauded?

I think of Zora Neale Hurston, folklorist and anthropologist, who complained about singer-actor Paul Robeson turning the spirituals into concerts. To her, he had taken the spirit out of the songs by *performing* them instead of *singing* them; he had transformed feeling that emerges from the heart, which cannot be duplicated, into feeling that can be constructed through art, which means that it can be duplicated on demand. One is genuine; the other is genuinely constructed. Hurston preferred the sounds emitted by the folks who couldn't compete and sing in the gospel choir or any other choir, but whose sincerity and relationship with God were apparent in their singing. These included those little old ladies who usually occupy what we refer to as the "amen corners." They are better at lining-out hymns, using the "long meter" that folks untrained in music historically make when they sing their joyful noises in African American churches.

In reflecting on this issue, I think of the Canton Spirituals, a family gospel group from Canton, Mississippi, and one of their most popular songs. It's called "Heavenly Choir" and it recounts the plight of an elderly deacon who is not allowed to sing in the choir in his "little church sitting down in the woods" because he is too old and his voice cracks when he sings. So the old man dies, is taken to Heaven, and gets his reward by "singing in the Heavenly choir." From that infinitely enviable position, his voice descends to lecture members of the church about their misguided understanding of what is involved in praising God. He points out that there aren't any divisions within choirs in Heaven—no Senior Choir or Young Adult Choir or Inspirational Choir. There is only the Heavenly Choir, and everybody who makes it to Heaven sings in it. There are also no special times for singing, such as on Sunday or Men's Day or Women's Day; in Heaven, one sings when one wants to. How preferable to have permission from God to sing all over Heaven, at any time, than to be censored by a mere mortal church choir director and members at some "little church sitting down in the woods." Of course audiences become ecstatic when the Canton Spirituals include this song on their live programs. And they reject the injustice that led this deacon to die such a sad death. Yet these same folks listening to the Canton Spirituals are the kind of people who prefer the talents of professional singers to those of untrained, everyday folks. Ironically, we can sing about a problem, but we can't seem to resolve it in practice.

I can't carry a tune in two buckets, but I sang in church gospel choirs for years and made a variety of joyful noises. Now, in places like Atlanta at least, I would probably flunk the test for making a joyful noise. I am currently one of the non-select few, but I cling to the consolation that in the matter of singing, my ultimate Audience thankfully grades on the curve.

CHAPTER NINE

Changes and Challenges

THE YEAR 1966 brought changes into my life that led away from church for a few years, to college, and on to graduate school. During my senior year at Druid High School in Tuscaloosa, students were busily planning the graduation exercises as well as planning for college. As a graduation committee member who had been in the drama group for three years, I wrote the play that our classmates would present before our parents, families, friends, and the white school board officials on graduation night. I don't remember the title, but it was a futuristic conception that enabled some of my classmates, from the vantage point of a space outpost, to look back on the members of our class and see what wonderful things they had accomplished after they graduated from Druid.

Because I had worked for so long with the drama students, I knew which ones could act the parts well and I naïvely assigned them to the play. Little did I know that such assignments were considered honors bestowed upon students with the highest grade point averages in the class. I learned this in my trigonometry class one day when, instead of teaching for the class period, our legendary and infamous math teacher, Mrs. Hall, vented her anger that "someone" had dared give out parts in the senior class play to students who had mere C averages. Such flawed persons were certainly not going to represent our "cream of the crop" before the school board. She did not stop her tirade when I started to cry, and she never once mentioned me by name. It was a dirty trick, the kind some grown-ups perpetuate against teenagers. I'm sure her tirade grew out of some behind-the-scenes politics to which I was not privy, but I felt the brunt of it nonetheless. What I found most interesting about all the controversy was that no one ever offered to toss my play out and start from scratch. Oh no, the work was just fine; it was just that the playwright had no business taking a stake in her own play. I was supposed to just give my play to the class and faculty to do with as they pleased—which is what ended up happening anyway.

All the students to whom I had assigned parts in the play were relinquished of their roles, and the students who held the top academic positions were "properly" assigned the parts. Although my class rank would have given me a part in the play, I refused to participate. On graduation night, therefore, I was the only student with a yellow tassel, signaling my membership in the National Honor Society, who was sitting in the audience with the rest of the class instead of being on stage with the performers.

I credit this incident, which took up a goodly portion of my senior year, with putting me a bit behind in the college application process, but there were other factors as well. Druid had a hefty reputation for sending good athletes and strong academic students to a variety of colleges and universities throughout the South and a few places in the North. Athletes were easily identified and received all the help they could possibly have wanted. Exceptionally talented academic students also received plenty of help—if they had the right skin coloring. With athletes, skin color didn't matter so much. There seemed to be a general feeling that a young black male body in motion in sport somehow exempted it from the colorphobia with which other segments of our lives were afflicted; it was a way out of poverty and a way out of color.

If you were female and brown or black, however, you had to be a junior Einstein before the stacks of college applications would appear before you. I was not a junior Einstein. I was tied with my best friend for the fifteenth slot in a class of more than two hundred students. Now, I could conclude that class rank perhaps prevented the counselors from assisting me with college preparation as much as they did some other students; but at least fifty students from that class went to college, so there were a lot of students ranked lower than me who were helped. And I could say that poverty averaged in; perhaps they thought that my mother would not be able to afford the amenities for me to go to college even if I were fortunate enough to be admitted. I could offer such excuses, but I think color played an equally large role. As a brown black child, I was not among the chosen few. Although my intellectual exploits in elementary school had made me special with my teachers, that was not the case in high school.

At Druid High School, as at most such schools in the South in the 1960s, a pigmentocracy prevailed. Within these black communities folks were judged on the basis of gradations in their skin coloring. *Intra*racial prejudice privileged lighter-skinned blacks, then browner ones; blacker ones had to fight their way in all the time: "If you're white, you're right; if you're brown, stick around; if you're black, stay back." The pattern was clear from the colorings of most of the students selected to represent the school in any public way. They were usually lighter, unless their brilliance or other talent just outshone skin color. You could be a brown band leader, but the head majorette had to be high yaller. And most of her supporting cast were the same. I learned this when I naïvely "tried out" for the majorette squad. "You have such big, pretty legs," friends told me, "you have to try out." So I did. Trials consisted of marching and prancing the length of the gymnasium floor to some specified music and demonstrating your baton-twirling abilities. When the list of finalists was posted on a bulletin board in the gym, I think I ranked somewhere around sixty, which was at the very bottom.

Now, admittedly, with my sense of rhythm, I might not have had a serious chance of joining the squad. In the environment in which I was trying out, however, it was almost a foregone conclusion that my efforts would be in vain. No knowledgeable person offered to help me make my trial the best it could be. On my own I simply failed. That young brown and black girls in the South, already subjected to prejudice from outside of their communities, also had to deal with it *within* their communities is one of the ironies of being black in America. African Americans adopted the same schema for judging their own people that white folks adopted, so they discriminated on the basis of skin color. The pattern continued in some historic black colleges, for this was in the era when some of these schools requested that photographs accompany application materials. We all knew that those requests meant that we would be given "the brown paper bag test." If our photographs did not reveal us to be light enough, we would not be admitted.

Without any particular assistance from anyone, therefore, I locked onto the idea that I would attend Knoxville College in Tennessee. I had never laid eyes on it (and still have not done so), but the information I received in the application process made it sound wonderfully appealing. Also, Mrs. Bennett, my sixth-grade teacher, had moved to Knoxville to teach, and I had hopes of living with her and her family. In retrospect, I realize what a tremendous commitment I was asking from Mrs. Bennett. I was nonetheless devastated when she said that she would not be able to accommodate me. Not having any funds beyond what would be applied to tuition, I was unable to attend Knoxville College. To this day, I have not seen Mrs. Bennett again, and I am often tempted to write to the Knoxville Board of Education in an effort to locate her —if she is still alive—or someone in her family.

I had also applied to Stillman College because it was right there at home. Attending Stillman presented far less dramatic change than would have taken place if I had gone to Knoxville, so each day, for the next three years, I walked from the Fosters Ferry Road house to classes at Stillman College. I credit my status as a "day student" to the fact that I never learned to pull all-nighters or play cards, especially Bid Whist, at which most of my fellow students seemed to be experts. Although I had been a member of the National Honor Society for years, I was unable to get a scholarship to Stillman. I received grants, and I worked to pay for the remainder of my tuition. My work situations proved to be some of my most engaging experiences at Stillman.

Initially, because I had been exempted from first-year composition class, I was a student assistant to Lois Broady, director of the Freshman English Program (her husband, Knute Broady, served as acting president at Stillman). A white woman with a background in Nebraska and the Presbyterian Church, Mrs. Broady was about as liberal, in the best sense of that word, as anyone could expect. I helped her sort through stats about incoming students and assign them to various first-year classes. I helped her with reports and any other paperwork that she needed in connection with carrying out her duties. She, in turn, encouraged me to read in areas in which I had not read. This was 1966, so Margaret Walker's *Jubilee* was hot off the press. I read it at Mrs. Broady's suggestion and discussed it with her. I was delighted when Margaret Walker came over from Mississippi to talk with our first-year class.

Mrs. Broady and her husband were two of many whites in Stillman's historic black college environment when I matriculated there. I happened to enter during an experimental period when faculty and advanced graduate students from Northern white schools such as Columbia and the University of Pennsylvania heeded the injunction to go south and teach at a historically black college. The chair of the English Department was one such person, as were several of the English professors. In fact, I remember only one black English professor at Stillman during my first couple of years there. We also had an exchange program with Indiana University, which meant that one of my first-year English professors was white Donald Gray, a nineteenth-century British scholar, who came down from Bloomington. Two white professors from Columbia headed up the honors program during my first and sophomore years.

That two-year honors program was probably a model of its kind. Our teachers designed a program that led us to explore writers such as Dostoyevsky and Camus in addition to British and American writers. We also explored important issues in society, such as increasing technological advances. *Lord of the Flies* was on the reading list as well as Machiavelli. We read Freud's *Interpretation of Dreams,* Plato, Sophocles and Petrarch, Martin Luther, as well as Karl Marx and Friedrich Engels's *Basic Writings on Politics and Philosophy*. We were nurtured and challenged to make imaginative leaps from our Southern rural environments into the larger world of ideas.

I could make that leap in terms of the assignments, for I read and understood them well. During this period, however, I discovered how painfully shy I could be in some environments. I, the tomboy, the public speaker in church environments since I was twelve, could not speak out in those honors classes. I read, I listened to discussions, and I wrote papers that my teachers applauded, but it was well into the second year of that honors class, when one of the teachers met with me and exacted a promise that I would say something in class, that I was finally able to break through. It took me a little less time to make the breakthrough in Donald Gray's class, perhaps because we were discussing *Invisible Man* and I loved that novel. Perhaps, too, my shyness was just from the knowledge that I was now in a world where most of the adults, ironically, were white, and I now had to speak before them; I had not encountered this environment before in my life. This shyness was something that plagued me for years, though few of my current friends believe it. I had to develop conscious strategies to overcome it.

I was not too shy to pledge into a sorority, however. Perhaps, again, that was because it was a mostly black environment. In 1967 one of my cousins, who was a Zeta, convinced my mother to allow me to pledge. All I would have to do, she assured my mother, would be to walk the line (agree to pledge and walk in single file around campus with other pledges during the probation period); she would pay all the expenses. Zeta sorors wanted me, but they also wanted my B plus average to bolster their academic record. So, to the shock of all my Druid friends, I ended up one day with a little royal blue-and-white ribbon pinned to my chest as an indication that I was going to become a Zeta. The friends who had come with me from high school to Stillman and who expected that we would all become Deltas never quite got over the shock. I can reasonably say that I was still in shock as well as I joined my one fellow pledgee in learning the history and secrets of Zeta Phi Beta Sorority, Inc., and as we went through the usual harassment that Big Sisters are allowed to inflict on Little Sisters. One of the milder ordeals included a command that we clean a Big Sister's room. We did . . . well, sort of, anyway. We learned quickly that the thing about pledging was to resist as much as you could the stupidity that Big Sisters tried to inflict on you. We "cleaned" the room, therefore, by sweeping all the dirt and trash under the rug. Given the state of her room, she probably didn't discover it before she graduated.

One of the events surrounding pledging that would ostensibly deny that I was ever shy involved the performances that each pledge line had to offer in the gym before the entire student body two times during the pledge period ("step shows" would be the comparable thing today). I cannot believe that I actually, with only one other person, marched into a gymnasium in front of hundreds of people and proceeded to sing and dance. I can't sing a note. Brenda was a bit better, but together we were just barely passable. There we were, in our glorious Zeta blue gowns, out of step (criminal offense) as we marched in and sang off key. I don't remember the songs (and don't want to). I do remember that the second performance was better than the first (we were obviously inducted into the sorority). I remember that the spectators were more shocked and encouraging than derisive. What in the world would we have done if they had booed? Once pledging was over, I really got into sorority life by becoming Basileus (President) of my chapter and by instituting various changes in how pledging occurred. I even got my mother to use her skills as a seamstress to sew the entire wardrobe of the first class that pledged while I was Basileus. Instead of the mourning black clothing that had been worn on the last day of pledging, we directed our pledgees to dress in striking combinations of blue and white during every day of their pledge period.

In addition to helping Mrs. Broady, I also worked as a student assistant in the dean's office at Stillman. I typed, filed, and answered the phone. I was typing one day when one of the white professors came into the office and found my skills interesting enough to stand over me and observe: "I can type better than that." So could half of the rest of the campus, but I had deliberately taken typing in high school and I was taking it again in college. I had been in my typing class in the tenth grade when John F. Kennedy was assassinated, so typing was something I was aspiring to be good at. And I eventually became good at it, despite that teacher's unsolicited evaluation.

The dean for whom I liked working most was Dean John Rice (father of National Security Advisor Condoleezza Rice). He was employed at Stillman just briefly while I was a student. A large, tall, brown-skinned man, he would sit and talk with me when our duties for the day were done. We had many late afternoon conversations about countless topics. I remember once, when he asked me what I saw my future looking like and I told him that I saw darkness when I closed my eyes to contemplate it, he said, "That's good. That means you can make anything of it you want."

It was during one of these conversations that I glanced at his desk and saw a wedding invitation. I asked him if I could take a closer look. It announced the wedding of one of our black male faculty members to a person who was not on our campus. "Oh my goodness!" I exclaimed. "I know someone who is going to be mighty upset about this." "Is it a student?," he asked. "Yes," I replied. "Tell her," he advised. And I did. In a pattern of black male faculty members selecting young black female students for sexual and other favors at historic black colleges, she had been "dating" this man for two years. He had, as Dean Rice and I suspected, been negligent in letting her know that he was getting married. She was terribly upset. Of course he didn't postpone his wedding. The most amazing thing about this development, however, was that he wanted to keep the student in his life despite the fact that he was getting married!

I had personal knowledge of what this man wanted, because one of the married male faculty members had approached me about becoming his little secret. As I was walking home from school one day, he had offered to give me a ride home (the practice was common in our community). I accepted, and he headed for a different direction than my house. He assured me that he just wanted to talk with me for a few minutes and that he would take me home directly. With some preliminaries, he got to his point: "I need a young stallion like you," he said, and I conjured up images of horses galloping over the range. He conjured up sex and the blues tradition of sexual "riding." This man had a wife and children and presented the perfect nuclear family to the outside world. Yet he, probably in his thirties at the time, was chasing a sophomore in the hope that he could join the ranks of his brethren who routinely acquired such students in their lives with promises of financial rewards. Was this any different from the prostitution that white men wanted from us?

These vultures were able to thrive because most of the girls in that environment had come from poor families. When approached by a slick black male teacher, some of them were not averse to spending a bit of sexual time with the teacher in exchange for much-needed items, even food. My mother's training would not have remotely led me to consider becoming a married professor's concubine, but I realize that I had the option of living at home, in a supportive environment. The experience of living away from home, family, and friends obviously played a part in some of these girls succumbing to the extracurricular roles the male teachers asked them to play.

Dean Rice left Stillman under strained circumstances when it was announced in the local newspaper (*before* he had told Stillman officials) that he was leaving to accept a position at the University of Denver. I remember him as a person of morals who encouraged me to think, to explore, to succeed. Our paths crossed again in 1989, when I accepted a fellowship to the Center for Advanced Study in the Behavioral Sciences at Stanford University. He had moved to Palo Alto, California, to be near his daughter. Ironically, I rented his daughter's condominium in the Pearce Mitchell complex on the Stanford campus. It was there that I experienced the famous earthquake on October 17, 1989.

Students at Stillman were tremendously politically engaged during the mid-1960s. A campus visit by social activist Stokeley Carmichael almost turned the place inside out when one of the professors, Mrs. Bennett, refused to allow Carmichael to speak in her political science class. Mrs. Bennett was a white woman who, for whatever reasons, taught at Stillman College during her entire career. She had two sons in Vietnam when Carmichael arrived on campus and found his presence and protest of the war an insult to her sons' very existence. She was not going to compound the insult by allowing him to speak in her class. And he did not. I was enrolled in one of her classes at the time and heard her explanation for her decision; others not so informed just maligned her. As a teacher, however, she was widely respected. If you enrolled in her class, you would be taught and you would learn. She played no favorites, and she would not tolerate less than the best performance you could give. She was a fixture on the campus. Carmichael was a disruption.

When he met with a small group of students, he asked us if we thought anyone could go to college. I was one of those who naïvely responded, "Yes." And there we were: goats for the objective lesson he wanted to teach for the day. Several students, including some who had come to Stillman from Druid, engaged in spirited conversation with him. One of them, however, observed that it was difficult to take Carmichael seriously because he had on a five-hundred-dollar suit and Brooks Brothers shoes. I had no way of challenging her evaluation, but it was good to have the campus settle back down to some semblance of normalcy after his visit.

Everybody remembers where they were on April 4, 1968, and I am no exception. I was home with my family when the announcement came that Martin Luther King, Jr., had been shot. Students on the campus went berserk. Student body president Michael Figures, who was later to become a state senator in Alabama, had the unenviable role of trying to calm the students down when he, himself, was just as angry as everybody else. The next day I was at the meeting where he pleaded with students not to march "downtown." What would they accomplish, and what point would they make by doing so? King was dead; if students persisted in the course they wanted to follow, there would probably be more violence and death. Finally, students were prevailed upon to plan a memorial service, and a few days later I joined everybody else in crying when someone sang "Precious Lord, take my hand."

I had seen marches in Tuscaloosa, so I knew that Michael's fears of violence were justified. When I was in the eleventh grade, I participated in civil rights training with my neighbors and classmates and joined them in demonstrating against restrictions imposed by local white authorities. We also demonstrated to get more people registered at the polls. We met every Monday night in the mass meetings that King and the black people of Montgomery, Alabama, had made famous in the mid-1950s. When we went out on our protests, we saw local grocery store owners don the uniforms of policemen and join in beating and teargassing us. It became a standing (gruesome) joke that the two Ku Klux Klansmen who owned a grocery store in the heart of our black neighborhood actually masqueraded as policemen.

The times were dangerous, but we fought for what we believed in. We marched and demonstrated, insisting that black people be hired in grocery and clothing stores as well as in other businesses, where staffs were previously all white (except the cleaning crews). We celebrated when the Klansmen who owned our neighborhood grocery store were finally pressured into hiring a black cashier (though she was rather high yaller). We happily chauffeured elderly people in our communities to the polls to ensure that they executed that hard-earned right to vote. Indeed, within my own family it was standard for the next thirty years that my sister Ann always juggled her job responsibilities on election day to make sure that my mother was driven to the polls.

During those marches I saw women like Mrs. Ostrean

Johnson, who, trapped in a church with hundreds of us black folks in 1965, dared to venture out, only to be beaten and thrown back into the church so that she could continue to be teargassed with the rest of us. As the teargassing continued, I saw a fastidious elementary school teacher gingerly dip pieces of toilet paper into a toilet bowl and wash the stinging, burning effects of tear gas—as best she could—from the faces of screaming young black girls. I saw the faces of my demonstrating high school classmates who had been chained on a front porch as a containment area until paddy wagons arrived to take them to jail. I was not arrested because my best friend and I, despite our training in nonviolence, outran the police and did not end up contained on that porch—or shot in the back and killed. The students at Stillman perhaps had no such memories to calm them down when King was shot. They perhaps had not seen firemen with hoses at the ready, waiting for black people to emerge from the churches from which they usually launched their marches.

King was killed during my second year at Stillman, which was really my junior year, in the semester before I went off on an exchange summer program to Indiana University. What I remember most about that summer was living in a dormitory in Bloomington, Indiana, with seven hundred students, only a handful of whom were black, and studying at least eight hours a day so that I would not embarrass the people who had given me the opportunity for this exchange. I was also shocked to discover that white maids cleaned our rooms and that some of the white girl students were sloppy beyond belief, perhaps because they knew someone else would be cleaning up after them. A dance provided the one extended break from studying that I recall. Each dorm resident filled out an extensive questionnaire and was then matched up, by computer, with a partner for the dance. I was matched with a white guy named Chris from upstate New York whose last name I can't remember and with whom I was never in touch after that summer. Since neither of us could dance, we opted to go to the movies instead. We saw *Rosemary's Baby*. After that outing, we just sort of smiled at each other when our paths crossed in the cafeteria. I think we were both surprised to learn that the more than eighty-percent matchup for us had been across racial lines.

Although my Bloomington experience was quite a change —and not exactly an unpleasant one—I was delighted to return to Tuscaloosa. Indeed, I had put up a huge calendar on my dorm room wall and had x'ed out the days one by one. It almost sent me into apoplexy when the Greyhound bus we planned to catch to return south arrived at the station already filled and we had to wait an additional two hours before we could start the long journey home.

Indiana University had at least given me a taste of what a nonblack educational environment would be like. It made me more emotionally prepared, though not completely, to enter The Ohio State University in 1969. After some initial trepidation, and even a threat to quit after the first year, I settled into that environment and earned the master's and doctoral degrees for which I had entered graduate school. To have done less would have been to fail the people who nurtured me in Alabama, and that was simply not an option.

Success, however, also meant alienation. Higher education for a person born to cotton pickers, I discovered, is another kind of tightrope walking in which one learns to balance the familiar and the unfamiliar, bare literacy and super literacy, working class and middle class. I did that in part by remembering one of my mother's favorite verses: "Whosoever you are, be noble. Whatsoever you do, do it well. Whenever you speak, speak kindly. And have joy wherever you dwell." It is not sophisticated poetry, but it depicts sophisticated human sentiments. Although I have not always been able to live up to the last two seemingly simple directives, they have always pointed me toward the values of people who may not have understood the theory of relativity but who knew that the reach of love could enclose education and geography.

CHAPTER TEN

Black Nerds

EDUCATION HAS ALWAYS PLAYED a big role in my family. My mother certainly inspired and encouraged us to achieve, and most of us did relatively well in school. "Get something in your head," my mother used to say, "they can't take that away from you." It took a couple of decades before I realized that my mother was supporting a money-making tradition, not an intellectual one. She, like so many of her peers, believed in education primarily as a key to upward *financial* mobility, not upward intellectual ability, though that was obviously a natural consequence. We were certainly supported in learning, and our parents were proud of what we did—to an extent. There was a general belief, however, that too much education created problems. Those problems might be manifested at the simple level of a cousin who didn't have any mother wit. Or, more dangerously, they might be manifested in insanity. I remember the first time I asked my mother if I could go to summer school in college; she was concerned that I was "studying too hard." This logic treated the mind as cotton picking was believed to treat the body; too much of it could lead to serious problems.

In retrospect, I think there was a general fear of the unknown. Few people my mother knew had even graduated from high school, let alone attended college and graduate school. There was an invisible wall in studying beyond which it was believed you shouldn't go. When I was in the ninth grade, my mother was proud because she could call me in to recite the Lord's Prayer in French for the neighbors. That feat was accomplished in recognizable school, for she herself had gone through the tenth grade. Once I started talking about attending school year-round or going to graduate school, red flags were raised. I would hurt myself mentally, possibly end up walking around talking to myself.

In terms of attitudes toward education, therefore, there was a sharp division in my community between the practical and the intellectual. There was lots of room for people who wanted to learn to become mechanics or electricians, for those were tangible, practical jobs that existed in the world. Mind work, beyond figuring the price of cotton or how to pay bills or the technicalities of being mechanics or electricians, was troubling, not well understood, and generally to be feared. There was a strange inconsistency in that persons educated out of practical usefulness still served as a source of pride to their families. Folks could respect you, for example, for earning a doctoral degree and could exclaim loudly to neighbors about your success; they just had little practical use for you and many times didn't know what to do with you. To become thus educated is to become a nerd, and black nerds are strange creatures indeed.

They are especially strange when their educational pursuit focuses on language and literature. Standard English, after all, was and is something with which many black folks have difficulty. To voluntarily elect to master that language and the literature produced in it set me further apart. Few people understood the desire, the pursuit, or the outcome. It was not something you could hold in your hand, like a screwdriver or a wrench, or the oil pan with which you changed your oil. But folks were indulgent, and certainly no one ever suggested that I give up the pursuit. What happened was that family members and men I dated were self-conscious around me. I would meet a new guy and, as soon as it came out that I was an English major, I would be greeted with something like, "I'd better watch what I say around you!"

The pattern was unwaveringly consistent. African American men are generally painted as being the ones with silver tongues, the ones who seduce women with the power of their voices, with the "lines" they develop in courtship. To meet a woman who specialized in language skills perhaps served to put their skills at risk. So they did the one-upsmanship and called out what was a source of disturbance to them. How could they seduce me with words, if I knew the words better than they did? There was little consideration that the arenas of talk were different. Their seductions did not come from the language of William Shakespeare and Ralph Ellison, and my literary analyses did not contain the lingo of disc jockeys. Yet to many of these would-be seducers, language was language and I was a threat because I was a master of it.

This pattern was particularly noticeable when I was in graduate school. A man I dated in Columbus, Ohio, for a couple of years and to whom I was engaged told me twenty years after our relationship that he felt so intimidated by my course of study that he would go to the public library in his free time and read while I was in class. He said he felt he needed to try to catch up with me educationally. While self-improvement is definitely admirable, this motivation for it was obviously wrongheaded. Because he had not shared this information with me while we were dating, it's a good thing we didn't get married. What in the world would that have been like? He did have a solution to my "overeducation," however. He said later that he had tried hard to get me pregnant because, if he had done so, then I would have married him. Thank goodness for birth control pills.

This man could only level the playing field and bring the nerd back into the recognizable fold of everyday folks by resorting to basic human procreativity. Anybody could engage in that. No healthy woman needed a Ph.D. to become a mother. This man, even though college-educated, reflected the attitudes of many in African American communities. Education for the sake of education was seen as a liability. Folks were not quite sure what to do with me, so they pushed me back into some recognizable slot in their minds that fit with popular conceptions of what black people, especially black women, should be and do.

My graduate school encounters with that ex-fiancé as well as with other men made it clear that nerd-dom is more problematic for black women than for black men. We admire those college-educated, professional black men who don their suits and march off to the workplace because we stereotypically imagine them married to women who are less intelligent or at least less well educated than they are. We consider women with comparable educational or professional training to be ball-busting types whose educations and professions frequently exclude them from romantic relationships and marriage. The opinion that I am too educated for most men, that I have "priced myself out of the market," so to speak, is a sentiment that has occasionally surfaced around the edges of my family. Few black men, it seems, are comfortable with the idea that their wives or partners make more money than they do.

While they can admire their sisters and other female relatives being so endowed with good fortune, they would rather it not reside in their own homes.

Receipt of the Ph.D. is the ultimate admission to nerddom. It is also the beginning of a lifetime of "set aside" experiences. Countless black folks who have been introduced to me over the years have immediately resorted to calling me "Doc." From their perspective "Doc" is a general title of respect, but I would maintain that it is ritual without substance, a game people play to remind you constantly of how different you are. "Doc" works as many of the interactions with black nerds work: it claims and rejects at the same time. It admits that you are well educated, but it also sets you up—constantly—as the noticeably different person precisely *because* you are well educated. You become the streetlight at the entrance to the community. It's obvious that you're there, and you may be something that no one else in the community is, but who the heck wants to be like you?

Compartmentalized relationships between black nerds and their communities are the order of the day. Take church, for instance. For those of us who grew up in fundamentalist churches, it is a constant challenge to retain some connection to them in our post-nerd-certified days. I know of no black church where the entire population is made up of nerds, which means that one or two of us usually end up in any given one of these churches. Immediately the "Doc" thing surfaces. You are first claimed with pride because you might add something distinctive to the congregation. Then comes the compartmentalization. Yes, you are well educated, but we don't really need your expertise in putting the newsletter together (translation: we really like those grammatical and spelling errors, or we don't even know we're making errors, or we don't want you showing us up). Why don't you just sit in the pew and let us point to you as one of our shining lights? Yes, you are well educated, but we're used to doing things our way on the Trustee Board. Why don't you just write a little article for the newsletter? Then comes a nerd standout day, such as Woman's Day or Youth Day, and the nerd is asked to provide the speech. For this set-aside occasion, it is perfectly appropriate for the nerd to have the limelight, because this is a onetime affair for which the congregation is seeking inspiration and words of wisdom that they hope will be derived from sources they do not usually consult, such as history and literary texts. Once the nerd has finished the presentation, he or she is expected to return to the silence of the pew.

Members of such congregations are always careful to be polite and welcoming to the nerd, and the nerd in turn is warm and magnanimous. He or she seldom gets involved in any ugly politics in the church. Instead, when they are there, nerds are the voices of reason in church meetings. Frequently, however, they are not around, because of their professional travel schedules, which means that travel in itself becomes another isolating factor in their relationships to such churches. For most of the members of such congregations, travel is confined to a couple of weeks of summer vacation. For the most part they are *in church*—Sunday morning and evening services, Tuesday night prayer meeting, Wednesday night Sunday school teachers' meeting, Thursday night choir rehearsal, Saturday morning prayer breakfast. To the folks who isolate the nerds, churchgoing is as much a religion as is their professed faith. The nerd not able to comply with that standard of performance simply reinforces the notion of strangeness.

Family environments provide another arena in which the

overly educated nerd encounters set-aside situations. Financial advantage does accrue to nerd-dom, and families recognize this even as they simultaneously have no idea why the nerd does what he or she does. Family members come to expect certain things of their nerds. Consider the situation of the Vanessa L. Williams character (Terry) in the movie *Soul Food*. As a highly successful lawyer of exceptional financial means, Terry is routinely expected to cover expenses that her extended family incurs. Yet she is considered too well educated for her own good, manifested in her inability to salvage two marriages and what others perceive as her general emotional coldness. Although the nerds I know do not have Terry's means, they are nonetheless tapped for a variety of family expenses. One fellow literature Ph.D. recently mentioned to me that she is expected to pay for her nephew's college expenses—simply because, her brother asserts, she can afford it and he can't. It's a logic that captures the usual contradictory responses to nerds. Even when you can't easily incorporate nerds—or reincorporate them after education "separates" them—into the family, they are nonetheless good for something.

Another nerd Ph.D. literature friend of mine is the only person in her family with that level of education. Her numerous family members in the Northeast insist that she visit them instead of them visiting her. They insist that she take their kids "down South" during summer vacations, so they can get a break from the little brats. Clearly this dynamic operates because of implied guilt. "You did well and we did not," this scenario might go, "so you owe something to the family." It's the mission versus money choice that has plagued black communities throughout their existence in America. When you have—or are believed to have—money, then your mission should be clear: give it in support of your family members.

My friends may not like being politely coerced with their finances, but they do not object to sharing with their families. The same is true with me. My mother taught all of her children to remain in touch with and to take care of each other. Anything that any of us can do for the others, we usually do. And, occasionally, we do it proportionately—folks who make more money pay for more of what is needed. Voluntarily assuming such responsibilities, however, is a far cry from family insistence on it.

The black female nerds I know are mostly professional single women. Some are single through divorce and others have never been married. A small percentage of us are married. I do not know that statistics on our marital status differ substantially from those of the general United States population, but there is a general assumption that the absence of male partners for many of us is more acute than with other groups. I don't think any of us wishes that we were less educated, but I would venture to say that perhaps all of us would like black communities throughout the country to expand a bit more in their receptivity to who we are and what we do.

Are we loved? Yes. Needed? Absolutely. Accepted? Always as intimate strangers.

CHAPTER ELEVEN

Fishing

AMONG AFRICAN AMERICANS in Tuscaloosa, fishing is almost a religion. That applies to the older people who love to sit on the banks of rivers and lakes as well as to the younger guys who trout fish in their fancy boats. The boat phase of fishing has evolved from the earlier bank-sitting stage, and my youngest brother, Eddie, and several of our cousins have followed this trend. When they were in their teens, they went fishing with their mothers and grandmothers and became fascinated with those slippery little creatures used for bait.

As a child, I remember my mother "digging bait" before each of her fishing outings. Nowadays, the men in our family have joined the ranks of those who search catalogs for the newest lures and who keep the specialty shops in business. Whereas fishing in my mother's and older sisters' generation was recreation that frequently served as a food supplement, today fishing is an art, an avocation that competes with practically any other high-priced pastime. In the 1950s my mother would go into the woods behind her house, cut her a "cane" pole, dig some wiggly worms, and head off to the nearest fishing hole. Today my brother hitches his eighteen-thousand-dollar boat to the back of his pickup truck (both painted black and white), loads up his paraphernalia (cooler, several commercially produced poles, an amazing concoction of lures and flies), and heads for some river or stream that might be as far as sixty miles away.

Though I have been fishing only twice in my life, fishing is in my blood. It's another of those things that my mother bequeathed to me. I therefore have a healthy appreciation for all fishing endeavors that involve everyday folks taking a day off from work and heading for some favorite fishing place. Tales abound about the location of the best backwater or the best gear to use. When I went fishing the first time, I was around twelve years old, and I accompanied my mother. Because she did not drive at the time, I do not recall how we got to the bank of this particular river. I do remember that my mother had to bait my hook (I am notoriously afraid of all manner of creepy, crawly things, most especially fishing worms). So I had the nice task of tossing the line out over the water and trying to follow my mother's lead in getting the best possible location to yield some plump, unsuspecting fish. I managed to snag one on that occasion. It was a smallish brim, about the size of my hand. My excitement, however, made it much larger, though I, unlike some of my relatives, do not tell big fish stories. My mother took my rather regular-sized fish off the hook (I can't stand to touch live, wiggly fish either), and I remember us celebrating the occasion. Later, after the fish had been cleaned, I ate my fish for dinner (don't mind eating them; just don't want to touch them while they are alive).

The other time I went fishing was with Ed. That meant getting out of bed at 4:00 A.M., going across town to get some fresh bait, and heading for some favorite backwater an hour away into which he could ease his boat as the sun came up. Though I cannot swim well (mostly I float) and Ed cannot swim at all, that did not stop our venture. We donned life jackets and went dashing around curvy river bends as he headed for some spot where the fishing was supposed to be really good. To get there, we had to pause at one point and open up a narrow passageway that beavers had blocked with a new dam. There was also added excitement because Ed had brought along his rifle to shoot any snakes that might have been tempted to get too close to us. Water moccasins are a particular concern in that part of the country. And Ed did get a chance to shoot at a couple of them. I marvel when I think that there I was, a nonswimming, nonfishing English professor, in some poorly charted waterway in Alabama, dashing about in a speedboat as if I were an expert. But I trusted my brother, and he knew every back road and waterway, mapped or not, within several hours of Tuscaloosa.

So we proceeded with our venture. Ed was nice enough to bait my hook and remove the fish from my line—until I started catching more than he did. Then he teasingly said that he was going to have to slow down the process of baiting my hook, because I was getting too good. Although I was definitely excited about catching so many fish, I was even more interested in hearing my brother talk to the fish that would potentially end up on his hook. One monologue went something like this: "Come on out, John. It's time for you to leave the wife and children. You know you want to see what the world has to offer today. Come on out. Check out this piece of liver I got for you. You know you ain't had nothing like this to eat in a while. Come on and get on this hook. Old Mary is sure gon' miss you, but I need you in my frying pan. Come on, John. What you waiting on?" And the conversation would continue with each fish. I would be cracking up, but he never missed a beat in talking to the fish, catching as many as he could, baiting my hook and his own, and unhooking the fish we caught and putting them in the cooler. I caught twenty-four fish that day, all of which I later packed up and brought back with me to Chapel Hill, North Carolina, to have my own little version of an Alabama fish fry.

I could not possibly duplicate, however, the art of fish frying that prevails in Tuscaloosa. When I was a child, we would simply cook the fish we caught in a cast-iron skillet. That cooking would occur at dinnertime, when whoever went fishing returned with a catch, or in the mornings for breakfast, when perch or brim or catfish would be fried and eaten with grits and biscuits. Now that fishing is more avocation than necessity, fish fries are social events, and the time, equipment, fish, and accessories are selected accordingly. The favorite fish these days is catfish, the result of an interesting development over the past twenty years. In many public parts of the South, lakes have been stocked with catfish to create "catfish farms," where the person who is more interested in eating than fishing can simply go and purchase already cleaned catfish. Indeed, some people have dug catfish ponds in their backyards. In addition to the catfish farms and ponds, the fish can be had from distributors who will cut it up into nice little "nuggets" that have quickly become the shape of choice. Fish fries, therefore, are elaborate affairs these days. They can be planned or impromptu. All that is needed is a few willing workers.

I have attended fish fries at which as many as sixty people were fed. The cooks might have two large electric fryers going in a carport, while four or five other people might be busy making coleslaw, hush puppies, french fries, or spaghetti and sauce (yes, I thought that was strange, too). Once the first batch of fish is ready, the cooking continues with the smoothness of an assembly line. Eating is informal—standing up or sitting down, indoors or outdoors—and conversation is always raucous and congenial. There can be fish fries to celebrate birthdays or holidays or engagements. When I brought home a new beau a few years ago, my sister Ann held a fish fry for us at her house so that everyone could meet him. He fit right in by eating as much catfish as the next man in the crowd. It was an occasion for the family to check him out, determine if he should be in my life, and act accordingly. I think he passed the test because he ate so much catfish.

Not only does fishing provide food; it also provides stories. The first fishing story I heard was a generalized one—not much plot, just a love of fishing. My mother told it about her mother, my grandmother Charlotte Ann. In the country in Alabama, neighbors were few and far between, so it was a general practice to have a few dogs around to warn you when someone was coming or when something unexpected was happening. My grandparents' heroic dog in this tale was named Hero. Hero would accompany Grandmama whenever she went fishing, which was just about every day, come hell or high water, and would stay by her side no matter what. He was her protector. Well, one day when Grandmama headed toward her favorite fishing hole with Hero jogging along ahead, she came to a spot in the road where he paused and would go no farther. He just barked and barked and barked. Finally, Grandmama came close enough to see what the problem was. There, lying across the length of the road, was the largest snake she had ever seen. Although fisherwomen usually believed that they had a divine directive to attack and kill snakes, Grandmama decided to pass on this one. She turned from her (almost) fishing outing and returned home. My mother would tell the story again and again. Hero was the dog with good sense, the one who saved his mistress and earned his place in family lore. Although that was not the only story Momma told about Hero, it was an impressive one. "Old Hero," she used to say, "now that was a dog."

While Grandmama might have passed up the opportunity to try to kill her snake, I am not sure my mother would have done the same. And perhaps that is why she told that story so much. It was a mythical lost chance for her to kill another snake. Because she fished so much on the banks of rivers, lakes, and streams in Alabama, her snake stories are bountiful. And she never backed away. My sister Hazel corroborates this. Although Hazel will pick up the worms that I won't, she will nearly faint at the sight of a snake. Momma, however, firmly believed in Genesis. If a snake was in her path, she believed it was her God-given right to bruise its head. And bruise she did, most often unto death. No matter the challenge, Momma killed snakes. None was too big. None was too little. She supposed that there was always a stick or branch strong enough and space clear enough for her to strike the snake. And, as I hear it, in some instances the poor snakes she encountered just wanted to slither away. Not a chance if they came across the path of Unareed Harris.

My mother was never bitten by a snake, either on a fishing bank or in the fields or woods into which she eagerly waded to wrest new garden space from the wilderness or to shoot a squirrel or rabbit for a hearty stew. I can only surmise that her quickness at snake-killing exceeded the speed of any snake. The most frightening tales she told involved coach whips, those constrictor-type snakes that would wrap around a person and squeeze the breath out of them. She had come across a few and had always managed to beat the devil out of them —again the biblical connection—before they managed to go into their almost always fatal coils. I conclude that my mother was particularly blessed, that her guardian angel, knowing that her children had already lost their father, was keen to keep a shield of safety around her to prevent her early demise from snake bite.

My sister Hazel tells the story of her and her neighbor Mary Stallworth going fishing with Momma on a creekbank near their homes. Mary had been sitting under a big tree fishing for quite a while when she heard a plop above her head. She looked up and saw that a huge snake had fallen from one tree limb to the next lowest one. She yelled for Momma, and the two of them got big sticks and started pushing and pulling at the snake trying to make it come down —so they could kill it. Meanwhile, Hazel says, she just sat on her fishing bucket a safe distance away and watched the drama. Momma and Mary kept after the snake, but they didn't have sticks long enough to force it down. They now recognized it as a coach whip, for it had wrapped itself tightly around the tree and couldn't be dislodged. Then Momma said, "I know what. Let's us pretend that we leaving. It'll come down then." Hazel says she had no idea that Momma was right, but once they packed their gear, gathered their poles, and started away, the snake slithered down. It obviously had not observed that Momma and Mary were still carrying their big sticks. They dropped their poles, advanced on the snake, and started beating it. Momma yelled out for Hazel to help. "That snake ain't done nothing to me, so I ain't gon' bother it," Hazel replied. No such sentiment ever stopped Momma. She and Mary beat the snake to death. When the snake was dead and Momma held it up as high as she could with her stick, both its head and its tail were still touching the ground. That means that the snake must have been at least eight feet long. Now, we all laugh when that story is told. I am puzzled, though, as to what led my mother to execute such risky behavior. Perhaps these adventures gave her after-fishing smiles.

For all her snake-fighting adventures, however, my mother was a staid fisherwoman. She could sit on the bank of a river all day, but she would not get into a boat—at least not until Ed finally convinced her to do so when she was well into her seventies. Before then, she would go with her fishing buddies, or one of her children or grandchildren, and sit contentedly waiting for some unsuspecting fish to grace her hook and dinner table. I always call my mother Champion Fisherwoman of Tuscaloosa, Alabama, and over the years I have dedicated books to her using that designation. Momma thought nothing of getting up at three-thirty or four o'clock in the morning, gathering up her fishing supplies and some meager lunch of a honey bun and sardines, and heading to the nearest riverbank until six, seven, or eight o'clock at night. There were times when she would be gone so long that I would begin to worry about her. After all, she couldn't swim either, and who knows when she might have slipped down a riverbank? But she always came home safe and sound, absolutely elated with her catch. She would be so energized from the conversations on the riverbank that it always made me curious about the topics she and her fishing buddies discussed.

Fishing was the site on which Momma exercised clear notions about how to treat one's neighbors (which didn't include snakes). I began giving her driving lessons when she was sixty-three, and the family bought her a car shortly after she earned her driver's license. Now she could drive herself—and offer to drive others—to her favorite fishing holes. So she would be ringing someone's phone in the wee hours of the morning looking for a fishing buddy, or someone would be ringing her phone. For the many years she had driven with other folks, she always contributed to gas costs. When she started driving, she always asserted that it did not take more gas to drive four people in the car than it did to drive one, so she mostly refused to allow her passengers to pay for fishing trips. I say "mostly," because there were a few occasions on which someone prevailed upon her to take a few dollars.

In the later years of my mother's life, fishing was fun—pure and simple. She did not need the fish she caught as a food supplement and would frequently give her catch away to neighbors or other family members. The only thing she required was that they do the cleaning themselves. Catching the fish had been sufficient pleasure for her. The smiles and laughter that would come when she described the pull of bringing in a larger fish or when she recited some venture at the riverbank were memorable. It was the family's duty at that point in her life to keep her in "fishing money." She didn't smoke, drink, or have any other vices. She just loved to fish. She loved the company of the women with whom she fished. She loved the outdoors. And she loved the satisfaction of a good fishing outing. It would keep her in smiles until, well, the next morning, when another fishing buddy called for an outing.

If ever any of her children were planning a surprise for Momma, they could easily effect it once she set off for a river-bank. There would be time to plot surprise birthday parties, which we did for her seventieth birthday, or have her garden tilled, or sneak in any number of other little treats. It was the time to bring in new clothes that someone had bought for her (practically everybody in the family shopped for her and could fit her almost perfectly). During one such fishing outing, one of my brothers bought Momma a new white suit.

When she returned and completed her usual after-fishing ritual (cleaning the fish, taking a bath, rubbing down in alcohol to dislodge any little creature that might have thought it had found a home), the new outfit was brought out for Momma to try on. It was absolutely gorgeous and a perfect fit. The story goes that she went next door to my brother Ed's house, pranced in, modeled the outfit, and said: "Give me a Band-Aid, 'cause I'm so sharp I might cut myself." It was a classic ending to a fishing day.

It is perhaps difficult for people outside rural Southern environments to understand the mystique of fishing along riverbanks, lakes, and streams. For the initiated, it is a pleasure that never grows old. For men married to women who are devoted to fishing, they become like football and golf widowers for most of the season that is warm enough to fish. For women like my mother, who were widows, fishing is the engagement that never becomes boring. In the nearly forty years that I was consciously aware of my mother fishing and her attitude toward the sport, I have seen her disappointed only when, for some absolutely unavoidable reason, she could not go. Never did I see her unhappy when she returned from a fishing outing. Instead, those outings energized her the way spinach was portrayed as energizing Popeye. It was like Santa Claus had visited and brought her her heart's desire.

It was most appropriate, then, that on the evening before my mother's homegoing celebration (that is, her funeral), her children, their children, and a host of relatives and friends had a catfish fry. We gathered in the house in which she had lived for twenty-five years and in which my sister Ann now lives. There were probably fifty or so people there. Two of Ann's friends provided the huge electric fryers in which the fish was cooked. Another friend had brought a cafeteria-sized pan of pasta salad. My cousin Joan, who is a cook at a local elementary school, donated huge pans of homemade rolls. French fries and hush puppies were also available, and soft drinks were in abundance.

Although we had just returned from the funeral home, making our final plans for the next day, there was no somberness at this gathering. Everyone there knew that "Miss Unareed," as I had now come to call her, had had a long and wonderful life surrounded by loving children and grandchildren. So we communed over the fish, remembered the woman who had made fishing legendary in our family as well as in her community, and were thankful that on such an occasion as this we could have sustaining, nurturing thoughts. No fishing snake stories emerged that night, but I'm sure at least one was in the minds of several people in attendance.

Fishing takes as much creativity as do the stories that are told about it. There is a tradition of fishing just as there is a tradition of storytelling about fishing. To be really good at either requires a devotion that most folks give only to their professions. For black folks who fish in Alabama, however, the idea of profession would be anathema to their love of fishing. Though much energy is expended on it, fishing is escape not work. Fishing is what one wants to do, never what one must do. What they bring to the tradition is an undivided love of entering the natural environment of those slippery little opponents and catching them in what they consider a challenging if not exactly fair competition. But then, what has ever been fair about love?

CHAPTER TWELVE

A Love of Expression

G ROWING UP in black communities in the South means constant exposure to words, phrases, and expressions that illustrate the creativity that has sustained a people for centuries. All my life I have been fascinated by the phrases and expressions I heard swirling around me that did not represent "book learning." They were ways of speaking that were passed down by word of mouth, in true folk fashion. I heard folks say, "Plague take it!" and knew that they essentially meant "Damn it!" I heard others declare, "Aw, the dog's foot!" when they were intent on not cursing. "I gave her a piece of my mind," someone else would say in describing how they "blessed" or "fussed" someone out. It's hard to imagine anyone parceling out their mind like pieces of candy, but that's the image that always came to mind.

Children received supplementary directives from parents to ensure that tasks were completed efficiently. For example, consider "no long 'liminaries" (preliminaries). A youngster whose parent has asked her to perform a task can be "mighty slow" in getting to the thing prescribed. A command to make the beds might be delayed with a meandering trip to the kitchen to get a glass of water or to the porch to play a game of checkers with the folks there. The youngster might respond, "I'm fixin' to do it," which has an uncertain future.

The beds will be made but not right away. "No long 'limi-naries" was designed to prevent the meandering, to let the person commanded know that the order meant *now, imme-diately,* not sometime within the next hour. It established clarity of expectation and left no room for the interpretive "I was going to do it."

My mother was the champion of such phrases. When she ate something that was especially delicious, or when she was thirsty and a cold glass of ice water really hit the spot, she would say, "That was right where Grandma hung her clothes." This expression tied together generations and taste. Because Grandma's clothes were appropriately "on the line" in that tradition of drying laundry outdoors, the phrase meant that something was exquisitely as it should have been, one of those instances in which reality matched perfectly what had been imagined.

As a youngster, it took me a while to figure out that when my mother said "dreckly," she meant "directly," and that meant "right away." I knew that when she said, "Get in this house, and no long 'liminaries," she meant that I should move "dreckly." I didn't have to interpret at all when she called somebody "an ungrateful heifer"; that described some-one to whom she might have given a hefty bunch of collard greens, from her own garden, which she had tilled with her own precious hands, and the person didn't even have the good sense to say "Thank you."

Momma always made a distinction between folks who had "mother wit" and folks who didn't ("ungrateful heifers" didn't). These judgments seemed to come into play with women more than with men. Our cousin Ilene, who had gone to college, had no "mother wit" because, while she un-derstood books, she had little knowledge of how to dress. She would show up at our house with mismatched skirts and tops and with her slip (usually dirty) hanging an inch or two below the skirt. "She ain't got no mother wit," my mother would conclude. That would be the similar evaluation of someone who let her baby lie unattended overly long or who burped a baby in a manner that was more likely to strangle it than to release the air.

I recall one vivid instance of a boy having no mother wit. Anthony Graham, who lived near us, was probably around twelve at the time of the incident and was generally judged to be a doofus. He was awkward and a bit shy, though I remember him participating in some of our neighborhood games. His lack of mother wit came out when his mother, on her way to work one morning, directed Anthony to "wash the greens for dinner," which meant that he was to have them clean by the time she returned from work in midafternoon. So, left to his task, Anthony proceeded to the bathroom, got a bar of soap, went back to the kitchen, and scrubbed those collard greens like they were socks in which he had played nine innings of baseball on a red dirt field. The greens were crumpled, polluted, and totally unfit for cooking for human consumption. Anthony, to put it mildly, did not have any mother wit. And it's questionable as to whether his mother had any either when she entrusted the job to him.

At first I thought that to have no mother wit meant that these folks had missing mothers, had not been raised properly. Then I came to understand that it reflects that accumulation of experiences that people acquire through contact with those around them, combined with an innate understanding of how to exist in the world. It's a combination of nature and nurture, of what one acquires through formal education as well as through folklore. It is the experiential baptism that one undergoes by virtue of being a part of a particular culture. It becomes instinct, second nature.

Mothers generally felt that they had access to whatever space a child happened to be in, so there was no hiding from them. "In the [name of a place] I had business" was the phrase used to express the place where the speaker was going to deal with a problem. If you thought to escape a whipping by crawling under the house, an adult might say, "Right under the house I had business," and they would drag you out and whip your butt. If Mrs. Johnson felt she needed to tell Mrs. Davis off about her dogs chasing her chickens, Mrs. Johnson might say, "In her yard I had business" or "Right in her face I had business." To "have business" was to take care of something, right away, "no long 'liminaries."

Many times, my mother would judge things to be a "scanless" (a scandalous event). "Scanless" went by degrees of intensity of outrage. It was a "scanless" for a mother to leave her daughter's hair uncombed for four or five days. It was a bigger "scanless" for Lida Mae and Monkey, Joe Ruthie's alcoholic parents, to fight drunkenly from one end of our street to another. It was an even bigger "scanless" for Mr. Perkins, whose wife hired adolescent girls to help her with housework, to touch the breasts of one of those girls. That was a "shameless scanless," which made Mr. Perkins "a dirty scound," which was a cut *below* doggish. In college my brother Peter revived usage of the word to tease my mother: "Momma, it's a 'scanless'; they cussing on TV."

Expressions might also be used to put people in their place if they were putting on airs. If someone got a new dress and went prancing down the street in a showing off mode, my mother might say, "Why she tryin' to show off? Actin' like she somethin' when she ain't got eyewater to cry with." No "eyewater to cry with"—that was pretty bad, sort of like not hav-ing "a pot to piss in or a window to throw it out of." That people so circumstanced would try to lord something over other folks was totally unacceptable. They had to be brought down "a button hole lower," and Momma was one of those folks who understood the locations of buttons. She sewed most of her clothes and ours too, so she could bring neigh-bors down a button hole lower if they tried to get too uppity. She could also bring her children down a button hole lower if we acted out. If that didn't work right away, she could al-ways threaten to "snatch a knot" in us. Afraid of what our bodies would look like contorted in a knot, we gladly sought the lower button hole.

In our community when someone was "fit to be tied," that person had been exasperated to wit's end. They were "fit" (that is "ready") to be "tied" (that is, "contained in some way") before they hurt somebody or something. If a child had gotten on a parent's nerves just one second beyond the nine million hours they usually allotted to the wrongdoer, then that parent was fit to be tied with the child's behavior. When the post office didn't deliver this manuscript to a friend in Boston in the three days in which it promised to do so and instead took seven, I was fit to be tied. I was not going to go out and blow up the post office, but I definitely wanted to give them a piece of my mind. I never could figure out the ex-act origin of "fit to be tied," but I always thought it must have had something to do with the country, farming life. What farm animal might have become so outrageous under certain circumstances that it had to be tied up instead of running free? Were there instances in which animals had specific kinds of "fits," as in the stray-from-sanity variety? Might the solu-tion have been to confine them in a pen or use a rope and tie them to a post or tree? Certainly hogs and cows were as a matter of practice confined in this way, but I'm not aware of any unusual behavior that might have led to any additional need for such confinement.

What was definitely connected to farming was another often-used expression that measured the degree of exasperation or anger that the user might feel. If anybody, but especially a parent, asserted that it was "too wet to plow," you wanted to stay out of their way. The corollary to this was "too dry to hoe," which was all right as an expression, but it didn't bring the dread of "too wet to plow." This phrase implied that the person uttering it, having been provoked, was *planning* the moment when he or she would go upside somebody's head. It was futuristic vengeance. Or futuristic punishment. The person on the designated receiving end of the action would therefore have time to contemplate the consequences. For example, if Momma said, "If y'all don't stay outta dat street, it's gon' be too wet to plow," we had been trained to know that the line between action and punishment was about worn to a frazzle. We had a choice. We could continue playing in the street and risk the whippings we had been promised were coming, or we could stop playing in the street *now*.

In the farming life, nothing could happen in the fields when it was too wet to plow. Muddy clumps of soil would not yield straight rows even if plowing were attempted. Too much rain created a mushy, unmanageable mess that temporarily alienated land from farmer. Perhaps the farmers were annoyed that they couldn't get their work done. Perhaps they were frustrated to see newly risen crops move from center row to the muddy inlets in between rows. It was a damaging and potentially financially destructive situation, given the duration of the rain. Perhaps from this general context of a dis-

turbing situation, "too wet to plow" evolved to evoke connotations of the dangerous ground someone had tread on in
pushing the limits of authority or neighborly interaction. A
child could push limits by playing in the street. A neighbor
could make it "too wet to plow" by allowing her dog to
dig freely in someone's newly planted bed of verbena. "If that
dog dig up one mo' of my plants, it's gon' be too wet to
plow," which means that the punishing action could be
directed toward the dog (physical, such as throwing a newspaper or a shoe at him) or toward the neighbor (verbal reprimand, as in giving her a piece of my mind).

The state of one's sanity—or lack thereof—was also fair
game for folk expression. African Americans do not habitually
confine to mental institutions persons who are judged—
or believed to be—mentally deficient. Many such persons
remain in their communities and are incorporated into the
activities in which other persons "normally" participate.
However, descriptions of the mental conditions of such persons are at times humorously incongruous to the person's
condition. Such descriptions might include: "Her bread ain't
done," or "He ain't playing with a full deck," or "She out of
her tree" (which has interesting connotations of animal life).
"She stopped short of the end of the row" (the cotton-picking connection). Their humorous overtones not withstand-
ing, such phrases are seldom uttered to make fun of the
person referenced. They were and are creative descriptions in
a tradition that prizes language as much as it prizes the imaginations that shape it.

Good Christian people are supposedly not to cast aspersion on any of their fellow human creations, at least not most
of the time. Every now and then, however, they just can't
resist temptation. Some positively unattractive person comes

along and evokes the response, "He a hun" or "She a hun." Now, I had been trained to understand that the person so labeled was being judged to be ugly (seriously ugly), but I had no idea how the "hun" business entered into the equation. Of course I later learned who the Huns were and what ugly actions they had executed, but it was still unclear as to how cotton farmers in Alabama might have adopted that comparison. Thus, as with any good joke, context was more important than history of explanation, so I contented myself with the prevailing contemporary intention and outcome.

It was only slightly less puzzling when someone declared that x person had "gone to Halifax." "Momma, where Miss Johnson?" "She gone to Halifax," which meant that she had gone on a long, long trip (by our standard of measurement) to some not necessarily specified place. It was one of those out-of-sight, out-of-mind kinds of things about which we should no longer worry our little heads. But if you asked, "Momma, where the rest of the tea cakes?" and she responded, they "gone to Halifax," you could forget it. All the tea cakes had been eaten and you weren't going to see any more until Momma made the next batch, which probably wouldn't be for another week or so.

The Halifax connection was more logical than the Hun one when I came to know of Halifax, Nova Scotia, and that some persons of African descent in the United States had migrated there during the nineteenth century. Could it have been remotely possible that at least one of those persons had come out of Alabama and left his relatives with the information that he had "gone to Halifax"? When he did not return, could the story have spread through his extended family and neighbors? Could it then have joined Southern lore as an expression for disappearance, absence, no return? By the time my mother used the phrase, it had become disembodied from whatever original context it had, but it had retained a connotation of travel, absence, or ending. I continue the travel mode of its usage by posting on my office door after spring commencement the following notice: "T. Harris has 'gone to Halifax.' She will return on the first day of fall semester classes" (at shorter vacation intervals, I've "gone fishing."). More than one student has stopped by my office in the fall to ask how I enjoyed my summer in Nova Scotia.

One of my mother's expressions, though, has puzzled me throughout the years. She used to say, when someone had done her wrong or didn't act neighborly or otherwise offended her, that she would "pass them like Christ did Cicero" (if "feeding them out of a long-handled spoon" didn't work). I knew pretty well who Christ was, but who the heck was this Cicero character? In context, I quickly surmised that my mother meant that she would pay the offender no mind, act as if their misdeed had had absolutely no effect on her. So I learned how to "pass" mean-spirited or mean-doing people "just like Christ did Cicero."

Later in life I continued to puzzle over this Christ/Cicero connection. Historically, they did indeed "pass" each other, nicely dividing the non-Christian era from the Christian one. But my mother had no historian's spyglass through which to view her use of the phrase. And she did not pause to think about the clash of secular/sacred, pagan/Christian ideas with which she was saturating her behavior. And her behavior itself—dismissing rather than forgiving someone who sinned against her—was not exactly in keeping with her professed Christian beliefs. Yet I thought—as I am sure she did—that the phrase and the action were not only both wonderfully appropriate but also justified. Those folks, we believed, deserved precisely that behavior from her and, as I inherited her line of reasoning, from me too.

Christ. Cicero. Christian. Pagan. Do unto others . . . What does all this mean? I locate my response to that question in the context of Christmas and how Americans routinely celebrate that holiest of holidays. We are a jumble of human beings at a particular moment in history, one in which Christ and what many would view as Cicero, or money-changer commercialism, are not passing by each other. Christ inspires Christmas, but concepts identified as "Cicero" apparently take over with all the commercial bells and whistles. More and more, it seems impossible to separate what's spiritually religious from what's socially pursued. It's hard in these commercial times to tell where "Cicero" ends and Christ begins.

Beyond the commercial the majority of us expect Christmas and Christianity to "pass" all other religious observances every December, for we believe that they smack of paganism, or at least of something of which we do not approve. As professing Christians, it should be tremendously difficult for us to "pass" the human Ciceros we identify as sinning directly against us. In theory, it should be easy for us to embrace difference, love our neighbors as ourselves, and pray for those who use us. Yet we find ourselves mired in judgmental name-calling and divisive separation.

My mother certainly didn't contemplate these connections. When she and I "passed" various Ciceros in the small annoyances of life, we were responding to small inconveniences and unacceptable attitudes. It was a slight lapse for both of us from our professed Christian beliefs. As I think back to those days, I realize that we were, most of all, mutually celebrating a love of language, a love of expression that encapsulated a given situation and context and crystallized it in a small package of words. Those words, like so many of the others that my cotton-farming relatives used, made poetry out of life, squeezed art from the cotton bales, and lifted imagination and storytelling beyond the confines of three cents a pound.

CHAPTER THIRTEEN

The Ubiquitous Hair

I F YOU WERE BORN black and female in the South in the mid-twentieth century, you did not have an option: you got your hair straightened. It was an uncomfortable and at times dangerous process to endure. Madame C. J. Walker probably had no idea what she inflicted upon thousands of young black girls who would have preferred *not* to have their hair straightened. However, their mothers had discovered the straightening comb before the kids arrived in the world, so there was little chance for them to resist until the "Black Is Beautiful" movement of the 1960s. Before that, however, you got your hair straightened or you were considered one of the oddest of God's creatures.

Hair straightening was a sorority into which many young girls had to be inducted kicking and screaming. Once there —once they had accepted the "norm" for black women's hair—most of them settled into membership in the sorority without too much complaint. I was one of those who would rather not have belonged. I hated to sit through the process of someone drawing a hot comb through my hair again and again, until it met their standard of acceptability. Transformative but not transforming, hair straightening was an ordeal to be endured. When I was an adolescent, my sister Eva frequently straightened my hair. She surprised me one day dur-·

ing the straightening procedure when she showed me both of
her hands, yet someone was still combing through my hair. I
jerked around to see that she had given the comb to a male
friend of hers, and he had been having a good time working
in my hair. At least he didn't burn me. Countless girls and
women were burned or scarred as a result of a hot comb coming too close to an ear, the neck, or the side of the face. Practitioners who could mostly avoid causing such injuries were
considered "good," and they never lacked for clientele.

Because hair straightening was a portable profession, it was
also something with which many black women supplemented
their meager earnings from a "regular" job. That practice is
still common today, though it is usually perms or braids that
find their way into the kitchens and living rooms of women
after they have left their weekday jobs or on weekends. Because the incomes of many of the potential clients might have
been insufficient for them to go to the regular shops, these af-
ter-hours hairdressing opportunities worked for them as well.
Today, however, women run the risk of encountering legal
problems for these unlicensed operations. State-licensing
boards have entered the arena of colored hair in an attempt
to regulate income that would normally be subjected to state
tax. It is an ironic turn of events, to say the least, because
members of these impersonal boards could probably care less
about black women or their hair.

Yet hair is nonetheless one of the sites of curiosity between
blacks and whites. Each wonders how the other manages with
her God-given tresses. Because touching across racial lines
was historically not generally allowed, it was hard for the curious to satisfy their curiosity. Some were just blatant about it.
For example, when I was in Tuscaloosa one summer using the
library at the University of Alabama and had taken my god-

daughter, who was around six at the time, to the library with me, one of the white librarians became fascinated with her hair. "Oh, it's so long," she said. "How do you take care of it?" She kept getting closer and closer as we sat at a table in the library until she did what she wanted to do all along. She touched the child's hair. "It's so soft!" she exclaimed, as if she expected to encounter steel cables. Her surprise has stayed with me all these years. It announced a short-circuiting of some expectation that she had brought to this exploration. Her tone conveyed that what she found was quite different from what she expected.

At the time of this encounter, I had my hair in a geri curl that I deliberately allowed to dry out as much as possible to imitate an Afro. At Stillman College and at Ohio State University, I had worn an Afro that was the style of the day. I kept length in it by braiding my hair every night or every other night, which was a royal pain. That, however, was the least of my worries with an Afro. It was interpreted as a political hair style, one that designated the wearer as a militant, ball-busting type. Now some women who wore Afros were militant but certainly not all of us. It was sad to see militant lighter-skinned blacks trying desperately to keep Afros when their "good" hair just swayed and sank back to their heads. They had few of the braiding or other upkeep problems that folks with more naturally kinky hair had.

Getting a geri curl meant slightly less care, but it meant you were also more likely to have greasy collars and pillows. Then, too, there was the issue of chemical processing. A geri curl was not unlike what black men had gone through for decades in getting "processes." It was still an unnatural way of treating black hair. Depending on the grade and texture of the hair, the process might cause the hair to fall out or some other problem.

Black hair care is an endless preoccupation, and there are several magazines and Web sites nowadays that address it, not to mention the huge numbers of companies that produce black hair care products (many of them white-owned). From braids to weaves to shocking shades of coloring, black women are always doing something to their hair, and at very regular intervals. The industry is probably worth hundreds of millions of dollars in annual revenue. In the past couple of decades hair coloring has become all the rage with black women. When certain well-known public black female figures became "blondes," so did many young black female imitators. The first time I saw a black woman (a really dark-skinned black woman) with platinum blond coloring in her hair, it gave me pause. Not only was it a shockingly incongruous picture, but it was even more shocking to contemplate what it meant in terms of that person's self-definition. It was also an indication of what I take to be a truism: people who love you will sometimes lie to you. They will occasionally tell you—perhaps because they feel you desperately need to be told—that something looks good when it really makes you look like a buffoon. If indeed someone earnestly believed the woman looked good, then something is seriously wrong with how women of African descent in America know and name beauty.

I have been in beauty shops where women were planning to spend eight to twelve hours to have elaborate patterns of braids created in their hair. Fake hair extensions are often added to these braids, despite the fact that some of this hair looks so unnatural when attached to a live human head.

Other hair extensions that are avowedly made from human hair blend in better but still may create a distracting pattern. Let's say that the black woman wants the long look. She will have braids of four to six inches against her head and then long tresses cascading down her back in a constant reminder that she wishes to imitate her oppressors—or at least be something other than what she is. This "bleaching out," so to speak, is a contrast to the women who braid in patterns that they claim are African-derived. Both styles are aiming for the same result—that is, lesser attention to hair—but with dramatically different outcomes. One signals a deep identity crisis while the other signals deep racial and cultural pride.

For all this attention to hair, however, the sad truth is that the styles with which black women adorn their hair have not, during the course of their tenure in America, made black women any more desirable in that grand scheme of beauty by which American women are generally judged or any more acceptable to the larger public. Bo Derek might have made braids fashionable beyond black communities for a while, but it was a short while. White women traveling south of the United States might get their hair braided in various countries, but they never keep the braids for more than a few days once they return to the United States; their bit of exoticism never turns into permanent change. Although I am not suggesting that *all* black women are trying to create white acceptance by mutilating their hair, I maintain that some of them are. Black women show that mutilation goes from the outside of the head to the inside, from their physical appearance to the way they conceptualize themselves. And for all this mutilation, they are still viewed as black women in a society that does not value them and that will never use them as the standard for beauty.

My search for the right—or at least the most comfortable —hairstyle has been continuous. I had one traditional perm in 1982 and knew that that was not the way I wanted to go. I sat for six hours once and let someone braid my hair, then took out all the braids less than a week later. So, in 1993 I decided to grow dreadlocks. No, it was not a midlife crisis. I was tired of chemicals in my hair, and I decided to get them out —permanently. I figured that if the chemicals were giving hairdressers lung cancer, then what the heck were they doing to me? I elected dreadlocks. You would have thought that I had shot the Pope. Friends were cautious, some family members were shocked, and everybody was skeptical of what the result would yield. Colored folks in the South are just not ready for "natural" hair that is *that* natural. They have spent too much time in the "fried, dyed, and laid to the side" tradition of hair care.

To begin properly, I had to cut my hair down to new growth, wet it, oil it, and play with it every day. I looked like a reject from the Little Rascals television show as I pulled on the nubby short hair to encourage it to divide into neatly apportioned sections and to stick together. That's the hardest time with getting locks, because every time I washed my hair, those precious little wannabe locks would unravel. At first they unraveled all the way, then after a few months the ends had begun to lock and held the new growth in its specific section even if it did unravel when washed.

It is an understatement to say that I had some curious ventures during this period. Mostly people just stared because I refused to take the option of covering my hair during this early stage of locking. Some people wanted to touch my hair —and many still do. They seem to believe that there is some mystique about locks that makes them pointedly different from other hairstyles. Locks also inspire unsolicited testimonials. Many African Americans came up to me during this short-lock period and declared how they would *love* to get locks, but . . .

Behind that *but* was the politics of black hair. One woman who stopped me in a grocery store parking lot in Atlanta wanted me to know how much she admired me for showing my locks in the less-than-two-inch uncertain stage. The politics of her job, she felt (though she had not tested them), would not allow her to do the same. Why is she worrying about it, I thought, when she has straightened hair that looks perfectly fine? Then she lifted her "hair" to reveal beautiful baby locks about an inch and a half long. She was wearing a wig until they reached a respectable length that would not draw as much attention to her.*

At least she was working on her moment of public exposure. Other women felt that their job situations made it impossible for them to wear locks. Several of them expressed admiration that I, a professor, was "daring" enough to have locks at Emory University, where I was teaching at the time. How did I achieve such a feat in that predominantly white environment? I didn't exactly know how to answer the question, because I had never granted to Emory the power to approve or pass judgments on my hairstyle. And no one at Emory had ever told me that hairstyle—any hairstyle—was a problem in that work environment.

---

* A June 11, 2001 *Jet* magazine feature story entitled "How Important Are Hairstyles in the Workplace?" described a black fireman in Washington, D.C., who was suspended for not cutting his waist-length dreadlocks; a black woman in Williamsburg, Virginia, who received a written reprimand for wearing blond hair (presumably because it was "distracting to co-workers and customers"); and a black policeman in Baltimore, Maryland, who was suspended for wearing shoulder-length dreadlocks.

I still have locks, and I still get interesting reactions to them. People still marvel that I have locks in the profession that I am in—though it is increasingly common these days to find locks in academia. Others find sneaky ways to touch them. Still other folks are simply complimentary. My family has grown to accept the locks. Indeed, the sister who was most skeptical about them (she thought they would make me look like folks she had seen in the media with three or four huge unwashed, uncombed locks) is now more adamant about me keeping them than I am when I mention that I might change hairstyles and cut them off. Upkeep, after all, is much more difficult than people would suspect. In fact, in the eight years I have had locks, I have had constant difficulty in finding someone to wash and groom them. One woman in a shop in Chapel Hill was audibly insulted that I even dared to call her shop and ask if such work was done there. For several months I went to a woman's house to have her wash my hair; for another several months a woman came to my house to perform that task. In the absence of a regular stylist, I returned to my "locktician" in Atlanta periodically until I was able to locate one within an hour's drive of my Chapel Hill home.

I can understand why white folks might be freaked out by locks, but I am constantly puzzled when some black people react negatively to them. It's a visceral thing, almost as if I have insulted them in some way. Maybe I have done something that they would not do. Have I declared myself an independent spirit free of social restrictions by wearing locks and am thereby somehow dangerous? A black friend of mine told me recently that her son, who is college-educated and an otherwise intelligent young man, maintained that he would never date a woman with dreadlocks. What is it about the hairstyle that makes some black people uncomfortable? I'm still puzzling out that mystery.

When I look into a mirror, I see a black woman with natural hair. It doesn't make a political statement or otherwise have a life of its own. It's a part of who I am. I wonder, though, what a black woman with "blond" hair sees when she looks into a mirror. Is she fantasizing about escaping her black skin? Is she imagining transformation that a straightening comb could not accomplish? Or is she just lost in viewing herself through the eyes of people who do not have her best interests at heart? What is it black women are trying to do when they want to escape being "nappy" and black? Or, if they feel as I do that their "hair" is just a hairstyle, then what mental feats have they undergone to arrive at that seemingly innocuous and perhaps erroneous conclusion?

Next to skin coloring, hair seems to be the perennial source of insecurity for black women. As numerous cultural observers, including Toni Morrison, have pointed out, black women "worry, worry, worry" about their hair. They curtail their physical activities because they don't want to sweat. This overconcern for hair, combined with fat-filled diets, can cause many black women to run greater risks of obesity, heart disease, and hypertension. They are always, as W. E. B. Du Bois pointed out about black folks in America, looking at their hair through the eyes of others. For every occasion black women feel the need for a new "do," one that they hope will transform them into something other than being black women in America.

And the beat goes on. It is not at all certain that passing time will show us a different rhythm.

CHAPTER FOURTEEN

The Price of Desegregation

EVERY YEAR a pattern is set into motion in January that continues into February. That is the time of year, as Langston Hughes would say, when "the Negro is in vogue." Or, to use the more contemporary phrase, when *African Americans* have lots of attention focused on them because of Dr. Martin Luther King, Jr.'s birthday and because of Black History Month. Although many of us keep standing up and asserting that we are black all year-round, it never seems to affect the programming in our communities, schools, colleges, and universities. So during January we dredge up all our memories and readings of Dr. King and blow our trumpets about civil rights and progress since Dr. King's sojourn here.

But every now and then, I want to say, Saint Peter, would you please pass me through to Dr. King? I want to bring him up to date on a little American and African American history. I would start off by telling him an anecdote about Zora Neale Hurston—just in case he hadn't gotten around to talking with her—and I would tell him about so-called progress in my hometown, what kind of impact the civil rights movement has had on it. And I would tell him about what a treasure trove of abuse has been heaped on him.

When the U.S. Supreme Court's decision on desegregation was passed down in 1954, Zora Neale Hurston, novelist, playwright, folklore collector, and general preserver of African American culture, was one of the few national voices opposed to that decision. Desegregating schools, Hurston maintained, was really a slap in the face of those black teachers who had done a superb job of taking care of the minds and the development of African American children. Such a decision cast aspersion on their abilities to do well what they had long been in the habit of doing. Obviously, most people thought Hurston was crazy. They asked, How could any sane, right-thinking black person in these United States of America really believe that segregation was best for black people?

As early as the mid-1960s, careful observers began to see some of the negative effects of desegregation, and if they had ever heard of Zora Neale Hurston, they probably would have discovered that they shared a lot in common with her. Those institutions that many black people held dear—the schools that three and four generations of their families had grown up in, the churches where their great-grandparents had been baptized—were gradually being destroyed or relocated. Many of these blacks discovered, therefore, that they were equal enough to be singled out as losers.

Consider my hometown of Tuscaloosa, Alabama. In Tuscaloosa, which is commonly called the Druid City, Druid High School had evolved from Industrial High School, which had been founded in 1944. Its principal, McDonald Hughes, had guided its growth into a well-respected institution. Many of the teachers under Mr. Hughes's leadership and example-setting had earned their master's degrees, and several of them were on their way to earning doctoral degrees. They studied at schools such as Columbia, Indiana University, and Northwestern. They were practiced in the art of education as well as in the art of discipline (no small feat in a school of sixteen hundred students).

Then along came the civil rights movement and desegregation. In 1971 the school was desegregated, which meant that a certain number of black students and teachers were transferred to the formerly all-white high school across town and an equal number of white students and teachers were to come to Druid. A fascinating dynamic was set in motion. Teachers from Druid with twenty and thirty years of experience and near doctoral degrees were sent to the formerly all-white school. Druid in turn got wives of white law students at the University of Alabama who needed something to do while their husbands finished their degrees and who had little, if any, classroom experience. Picture, then, a petite blond woman coming into a classroom of primarily black students, many of them athletes towering over her. When she says, "Please take your seats," they respond, rather gruffly, "Who you talking to?" and she wilts into silence. From that moment forward, she has no control over the classroom, and no learning occurs.

The so-called exchange was a fiasco. The former white school became solidly integrated; the former black school ended up with a few white teachers and a few white students. Most of the white parents responded by sending their children to recently established "Christian" and other private schools in order to avoid sending them to Druid (a common story in countless cities during this period). Consequently, a move was started in the late 1970s to turn Druid into the lower division of the senior high school. All tenth graders throughout the city would go there; it would now be called Central West. All eleventh and twelfth graders would go to the former white high school, which would become Central East. Central East would have the basketball and football teams, the cheerleaders and the symphony orchestra, and all the other things that make high school extracurricular activities interesting. Druid would simply be the holding pen for those students waiting to go to Central East.

Needless to say, those of us who graduated from Druid High School between 1944 and 1970 were not thrilled with these developments, but we lost in our fights with the Board of Education as well as with the city. Today we still have our two schools, and the Dragons, the former mascots of Druid High School, are in hibernation. We are still curious to see if we will get museum space for our mementos. We still wear our red and blue and refer to the upper-division school in our community as Druid High School. All of the black kids who have graduated from that school in the past thirty years similarly refer to it as Druid High School. It's sort of like the situation in Toni Morrison's novel *Song of Solomon*. Although the white folks change the name of the major street in the black neighborhood from "Doctor Street," because the town's only black doctor lives there, to "Mains Avenue," the black folks retort by calling it "Not Doctor Street." Black reality prevails.

I moved away from Tuscaloosa in 1969, but I return three, four, and sometimes as many as five times a year. It is not only home for me; it provides a fascinating study in the consequences of so-called integration, of the impact that the civil rights movement has had on black culture, on the people and the institutions instrumental in the shaping of values within and among black children. I valued the time when teachers were surrogate parents, when neighbors felt a responsibility in the shaping of a child's growth. Now the schools have changed, and the old neighborhoods have given way to shopping centers and freeways. I valued the time when Mrs. Sawyer, the fifth-grade teacher at Thirty-second Avenue Elementary School, came to see my mother because my brother had been naughty in school (she lived only two blocks away). I valued the time when my aunt—though I never could figure out exactly how she was related to me—would admonish me to sit or otherwise behave like a young lady. I valued the time when you could work for your teacher if she was having a club meeting and make a few extra dollars, or when a teacher would come to your house if you were ill to see how you were doing, or bring a bolt of cloth for your mother to make new dresses for you if you could not afford to buy new ones. I do not wax romantic. I merely paint a picture of the way things used to be before we decided that so-called integration was better, before our teachers moved out of our neighborhoods, and before disciplining a child became a criminal offense instead of neighborly intervention.

There is a price for change, and black people throughout this country have paid the price of desegregation. Don't misunderstand me; I am not suggesting that it was the wrong step to have taken at the time. And please do not class me with whites who advocate maintaining the purity of ethnic neighborhoods. What I am suggesting is that few, if any, African American individuals ever stopped to think through some of the potentially destructive consequences of desegregation. They never stopped, for example, to think what desegregation would do to black schools and colleges. The general feeling was that the meeting of black and white would be glorious; we would all join hands and traipse off into the sunset together, in a vision that would have been the envy of the Communist party of the 1930s. But something else happened. There was a great gap between what was taken away and what was put in its place. The schools and colleges that had given the world the likes of Booker T. Washington, George Washington Carver, James Weldon Johnson, and Dr. Martin Luther King, Jr., were now looked on with suspicion. "Go to a black college?" some of our misguided young minds would question, "Why, only the folks who can't get into white colleges go to those things."

One of the negative consequences of the civil rights movement, therefore, was that it taught some black people—and I emphasize *some*—to disparage their own roots. I maintain that we have lost a couple of generations of young black people who are insensitive to their history and to their ancestors. I keep coming across junior high school students who have gone to their integrated schools and who don't know any of the names I just mentioned. I keep coming across black college students who never heard of Brer Rabbit and the Tar Baby, or of John and Old Massa, or of John Henry. And indeed, many of the junior and senior high school students sometimes cannot relate a single piece of factual information about Dr. Martin Luther King, Jr. Although I am sometimes surprised and always saddened by these revelations, I am more often angered. I am angry with the teachers who would prefer babysitting to teaching. I am angry—even as I understand—that many black parents are afraid to meet with white teachers about their children's performances in classrooms. I am angry with all the circumstances that none of us, individually, can control, but for which all of us, collectively, are responsible.

Although I obviously cannot advocate returning to those days before 1954, I can certainly understand Zora Neale Hurston's point of view. She had the foresight to see some of the things that others are only now becoming aware of. It is a fact that we have achieved a lot of vertical integration; we eat in the same dining halls, sit in the same classrooms, and sometimes chitchat about things of no specific consequence to either blacks or whites. Our relationships are still too fragile to be tested in the fire of amicable but serious disagreement. So we operate at a surface level that is a mere tranquil covering for the boiling depths beneath. And I ask myself, Is this what Dr. King wanted? I imagine myself talking to him sometimes. Black folks, after all, have a long history of dealing with Saint Peter. He is a constant character in our folk narratives about Heaven. So he lets me through.

"Excuse me, Dr. King," I say, "but it's January again, and you're being whipped again. For the past two weeks I have heard more boring speeches and platitudes in your name than the law allows. And they are usually so solemn and *un*-eloquent, not at all like anything you would ever say or anything that would ever appeal to you. The speechifiers paint you as serious, serious, serious, without even a hint of the sense of humor that I know you had. They believe that you were an activist twenty-four hours a day, walking five feet above the soil on which the rest of us tread heavily. They lament what they call the tragedy of your life, your early death, without ever considering the fact that your view of the situation might have been entirely different. People take out their handkerchiefs, shed a few tears, and convince themselves that they are somehow in touch with you. Sometimes it gets to be disgusting, but it's sort of un-American for anyone to say that out loud.

"In every city worth its name in the United States, you are being taken out of musty drawers and called into action again. Doesn't it just make you mad? Every petty city official from Maine to California and from Michigan to Florida thinks he can increase his black vote by mentioning your name. It would be great if half of them meant it. But they drag out your name as if you were some magical potion, then they chant a few syllables and put you away until the next year.

"And black folks are no better. Every year, the society ladies and their clubs sell tickets to some fancy dinner where all the people who think they are somebody come to show off their finery. I went to one of those recently, but not because I had any finery to show off. I paid one of my fraternity brothers fifty dollars for two tickets because I was his soror and he needed my support. The dinner was supposed to start at 7:00 P.M. At first, we were delayed because some of the *stars* hadn't shown up; then, when they got there, we were delayed another twenty minutes or so because all the folks scheduled to sit at the head table had to be properly lined up—according to somebody's sense of their self-worth. Then the mistress of ceremonies had to introduce the twenty-some folks at the head table, after which they started speechifying. By the time somebody realized that this was a banquet, and that we were supposed to be eating, it was 8:15. Then dinner was spoiled throughout by people getting up and mouthing off platitudes. I don't know, Dr. King, but it seemed to me that you would have preferred to be remembered in some other way.

"And have you noticed how city administrators use you as a pacifier? Have you looked at any maps recently and seen how many streets in this country are Martin Luther King, Jr., Roads, or Boulevards, or Avenues? Or elementary schools or cultural centers? And have you noticed where those streets, schools, and institutions usually are? One thing's for sure; they're seldom—if ever—in those sections of town where the lawns are perfectly manicured and eighty-thousand-dollar cars grace the driveways. Practically every street they ever named after you, Dr. King, is in a predominantly black, segregated neighborhood. That's not what you stood for, Dr. King. Does that bother you?

"And what about all those housing projects and schools? Have you observed how many of them have your name? I have never seen a King Heights, a King Club, or a King Estates. It's always a visible project with your name on the street that runs through it. And any time the black folks are screaming for more of whatever, they get a black school named after you. These schools are all over the South. Again and again, county commissioners and members of Boards of Education suggest that you were—and are—relevant only for black folks.

"Only when it's convenient do organizers of celebrations in your honor suggest that you have greater meaning. After that banquet I attended, everybody got up and sang 'We Shall Overcome.' It was dead and dry and perfunctory, but they tried, and at least the context was historically connected to you. Now gays, lesbians, and feminists have adopted the song as a rallying point. You've become such a handy catchall for so many things, causes, and groups that people tend to forget what you really stood for: the complete political, moral, and social transformation of America, especially in terms of racial understanding. You were not a mere token. I wonder if you're up there shaking your head in disbelief at all this confusion, or if you just turn away and refuse to look in this direction.

"Did you ever have any idea that schools in the South would end up the way they have? Do you ever have second thoughts about the tactics you used? Do you and Gandhi discuss these things? Do you ever want to be reincarnated and try to set the record straight?

"One thing's for sure, Dr. King; folks who profess to honor you have worn you to a frazzle. I think black folks and white folks—and everybody else who has become interested in you—ought to come up with some new names to toss around. After all, why must all the black folks' heroes be dead and martyred? Why can't we come up with somebody else who could articulate the concerns of the times? Would you like your name to take a rest, Dr. King? It's hard for people to give up their heroes, and I'm not suggesting that we forget you. But I do think that we should be clear in conveying to others that your dream of racial harmony and understanding almost forty years ago cannot forever sustain more than thirty million people. And if we're *not* going to give you a rest— and that seems likely—we ought to try at least to recapture your ideals in a meaningful way: work to make laws apply equally across racial lines, get more black kids adopted, and improve educational access for poor black kids."

Yes, I talk to Dr. King. I like to think that he listens. I like to think that every now and again he wants to say something back to me. But I think Saint Peter insists that the communication be oneway. That way, he doesn't have to mediate between disgruntled saints trying to come back to earth to straighten out the confusion that ensued after their deaths and supplicants on earth who would like that to happen. Not me. I don't want Dr. King to come back and have to go through this madness again. But I do think he should encourage the archangel Gabriel to hurl a lightning bolt in this direction every now and then—just enough to set a little fire under someone who will realize that saints are saints and that this world needs some flesh and blood bodies to carry on whatever battles must be fought in this realm.

If the consequences of the civil rights movement—those anticipated and those not—are ever to be balanced in some way, Dr. King cannot do it. The spirit of his work cannot do it. But perhaps, just perhaps, some of the people who keep standing on his shoulders and claiming kinship to him will find philosophies and practical ways to make "We Shall Overcome" an obsolete tune.

CHAPTER FIFTEEN

The Staying Power of Racism

IN 1970, twelve years before she became famous for *The Color Purple*, Alice Walker published her first novel. Entitled *The Third Life of Grange Copeland*, it is the story of two generations of black men caught in the mind-numbing sharecropping system in Georgia, Walker's home state. In a desperate effort to escape circumstances that have essentially turned him into an animal, Grange, the father, escapes/migrates to New York City around the fourth decade of the twentieth century. He does not find the promised land there; rather, he experiences an almost equally dehumanizing environment. He can't find a job, so he resorts to robbing and stealing. To retain some semblance of humanity and in an effort to remember who he is in this alien, psychologically destructive environment, he goes around repeating to himself, "Grange. My name Grange."

Let me focus on the moment in the text that drives him back to Georgia. He has been sleeping in Central Park and fits the profile of what we would call a homeless person today. One evening, he watches a scene unfold between a very pregnant young blond white woman and her soldier lover. Apparently the woman had trusted the man to the point of having sex and ended up pregnant, only to discover that he is already committed. He meets her in the park on a cold wintry evening to give her money, perhaps to leave him alone or to take care of herself and the baby for a while, for it is clearly too late for an abortion. The young woman, crying, angry, and distraught, drops the money and walks away. Grange can certainly use the seven hundred dollars, more money than he has seen at one moment in his entire lifetime, but he is shaken by the woman's plight, so he picks up the money and approaches her with it.

Initially, the woman denies that it's her money, then, contemplating Grange, she demands that he give it to her. She would rather throw it away—into a pond—after calling Grange a "big burlyhead" than allow a "nigger" to have it. After wrestling with Grange over the money, she falls into the pond. Here, I let Alice Walker take over:

> Grange had been standing mute and still, but immediately he raced down the shallow steps to try to reach her from the bank. In a split second he recalled how he had laughed when his grandfather admitted helping white "masters" and "mistresses" out of burning houses. Now he realized that to save and preserve life was an instinct, no matter whose life you were trying to save. He stretched out his arm and nearly touched her. She reached up and out with a small white hand that grabbed his hand but let go when she felt it was *his* hand. Grange drew back his dirty brown hand and looked at it. The woman struggled to climb the bank against the ice, but the ice snagged her clothes, and she stuck in the deep sucking mud near the steep shore. When she had given him back his hand and he had looked at it thoughtfully, he turned away, gathering the scattered money in a hurry. Finally she sank. She called him "nigger" with her last disgusted breath.[*]

---

[*] Alice Walker, *The Third Life of Grange Copeland* (1970; reprint, Avon, 1971), 161. Emphasis in original.

With the bills he gathers, Grange returns to Georgia and buys the farm that he will live on for the remainder of his life.

In reflective moments I can *respect* this young white woman for her refusal to bridle her tongue, for her *willingness* to die for the hatred she holds. She is immune to *subtlety*, that *disease* that I think so frequently clouds racial interactions in the southern part of the United States. She is, stereotypically, one of those white Northerners about whom we like to believe that they always let you know where you stand with them racially. She is *uncompromisingly* racist. Sad in a fictional character, even sadder in life. She makes clear the position from which I offer my remaining observations.

I am *not* interested in focusing on theories of race. I am *not* interested in focusing on abstractions or social constructions, about how people could be something else if environment and social forces would allow them to be. That may be true, but I am interested in the places, as one of my friends asserts, *where the rubber meets the road*. Where people in the small, everyday circumstances of their lives have encounters with racist people who have sprouted from racist environments and who basically are at home in those environments.

I *am* interested in the manifestations of racism at the level where people go to their jobs, interact with their employers and colleagues, eat their lunches, go on their social outings, walk through their neighborhoods, attend their churches, and generally go about the mundane business of their lives. I am interested in those moments when, at four o'clock in the morning, a white supervisor at the University of North Carolina at Chapel Hill can call a black woman a "nigger" and get away with it because he knows she has little, if any, redress, and he can always dispute her word. There is no philosophizing here, no abstraction, no social construction on the part of the black woman. There is simply the power dynamic that this white man believes accrues to him because of who, what, and where he is. It's a psychological power as well as an economic power. It is this level at which I reflect on negative interracial interactions.

However, perhaps I should pause briefly—in response to someone's thoughts—to say that things *are indeed better* for African Americans—*some African Americans, at least*—than they were fifty years ago. After all, I teach at the University of North Carolina at Chapel Hill and interact on a daily basis with folks whom I would not have approached on the street as a child in Tuscaloosa. Black folks are prominent in American society in any number of high profile places, and that has made lots of folks think that progress is truly great.

In addition, African American cultural forms saturate our media spaces, and that gives nonblack Americans the opportunity to think generously toward black people. Take black music, for example; it is on the airways practically everywhere. I go into my spa, and fully *ninety-eight* percent of the background music I hear as I work out is African American, from Smokey Robinson to the theme song from Shaft to the Staple Singers. In the malls in which I shop, the same thing is apparent. Television commercials are rife with such music. An airline ad even uses the soundtrack from *Space Jam*. And, nowadays, wonderful black voices are frequently the ones that *voiceover* television commercials. Stage, film, and TV luminary Ruby Dee tells us that New York Life "is the company you keep." Actor James Earl Jones wants us to know, "This is CNN." These are forms of what I call "invisible blackness." The nonblack American public will tolerate "blackness" more *in the ear* than *in the eye* (think of white suburban kids, in the "safety" of their homes, listening to black rap artists who spout lyrics directed specifically against them). So the public doesn't have to see James Earl Jones or Ruby Dee, and it can tap its foot or work its muscles to the spa music without giving too much thought to the musicians.

These are patterns in American culture, ones that I simply recognize and keep on seeing. Nonblack Americans simply can't tolerate too much "visible blackness." It gets to be too much. And because I am an academic, several of my examples will come from academia. In my thirty-one years of teaching in predominately white American universities and reading and hearing about others, I know of *no* non–African American studies department that has more than five African Americans in it. Usually, when a department gets one or two, it believes it has "diluted" itself enough—a little blackness, as novelist Ralph Ellison suggested in *Invisible Man,* goes a long way. These small drops of blackness are therefore always contained or controlled. I have no hope of this changing during my tenure in academia. But these are institutions, and I want to focus more on individuals.

For the past thirty-one years I have had countless opportunities to observe as well as be a part of *uncountable* interracial interactions, and I have formulated some categories to guide my analyses. The first of these is the *public/private* category. After the civil rights movement, after voter-registration acts, after integrating schools, it is hard to find many people like the unnamed young blond woman in Alice Walker's novel. Few people are going to come up to me and call me a "nigger." Indeed, the only time in my life that I have been called such—to my face, at least—was ironically in New York. I was on my way to the Russian Tea Room back in the 1970s when some white woman with a foreign accent followed me and a white friend for almost two blocks yelling out the word "nigger." At first we didn't understand what she was saying, and when we did, we laughed. The woman was so desperately invested in something that she thought would make a difference that she simply could not believe it when it did not.

So today we won't find any of Walker's characters or any-one like the woman I encountered in New York in the 1970s. *The law* and public opinion have made it clear that such be-havior is mostly unacceptable. However, it has been fascinat-ing for me to observe *what white people do when they are not being observed by their peers.* Again, these are sad examples, but they are nonetheless true. Over the years there have been white men in English departments in which I have worked who, when they were unobserved by other whites, refused to speak to me or acknowledge my existence. I remember how shocked I was when a white male colleague and I were both in our offices early one morning, long before others had ar-rived, and we happened to enter the hallway at the same time. "Good morning," I called out. He said nothing. Whatever excuses I might have tried to attribute to his behavior proved over the years to be irrelevant, for he had conveyed pre-cisely what he wanted to convey—that he elected not to ac-knowledge my existence *in those private moments.* The same was true of another white man. Yet, when these English de-partments held receptions and public gatherings, both men would join in groups in which I was involved in conversations and pretend that we had been best buddies for years. Both these men valued the opinions of their *nonblack* colleagues, so they toed the proper racial line among them. Yet their hearts remained unchanged.

The law affirmed that I could be on the faculties of these universities, but these men's hearts told them that I shouldn't be there. This was a psychological conspiracy that made me wonder how these folks treated the black students in their classes. But then I concluded, they probably treated them relatively well, for those students did not profess to be their equals. Indeed, if these guys had black people working for them in their homes, they probably treated them well, because there is also a different class and economic dynamic at work. And they perceived black folks who worked *for* them to be in their "proper" places in the racial hierarchy.

As a person who walks all over Chapel Hill, I am equally fascinated by how the *public/private* category operates in the wider world. If I'm walking on the street at seven o'clock in the morning or five o'clock in the evening, it's not unreasonable to assume that the white person coming toward me —similarly working out and sweating—is someone I might greet. Well, it's a hit-or-miss proposition that the white person will speak. Sometimes there's a response and sometimes not. People who ignore such social encounters and do not respond to being spoken to are operating—even though they are in public spaces—in the private arena. No friend of theirs is looking over their shoulders, so they can just be themselves. I *do not matter* to them, so they can exhibit even these small racist reactions. Perhaps you think I am overly sensitive? Perhaps they were just preoccupied? Perhaps their intentions were different from what I'm imagining? Thirty-one years is a long time to offer such excuses.

Such behaviors frequently backfire. On several occasions when people have seen me out walking and failed to acknowledge me, our paths cross later in "legitimate" social gatherings. At some reception or cocktail party, I look up and there is old so-and-so who refused to speak on the street. Old so-and-so turns beet red, then waits for an opportunity when several other people are around me, and comes up and says something like, "Don't I see you walking in my neighborhood? I thought that was you. I would have spoken, but you were working out so hard I decided not to interrupt you." Thus they try to smooth over our previous encounter. *Changing reality*—white people are as good at that as black people. Audre Lorde, famed African American poet and essayist, writes in her autobiography that her mother would declare that a windstorm had blown up when whites spit on them in New York in the 1930s and 1940s. So my neighbors change reality and *shift blame.*

My second interactive category is called *insiders and outsiders.* I teach in a predominately white university, and I doubt that there is a week that goes by without someone reminding me of that—sometimes in subtle ways, sometimes in not so subtle ways. I attend countless functions at the university, but I can always count on a particular pattern emerging. Let's say there's a reception or a lecture to which a whole host of people, including me, have been invited. I walk in and two or three white people—*not a single one of them the host or the hostess*—with eyes lit up in surprise, will walk up and say, "Thank you for coming." That sounds nice and polite, doesn't it? To me, that translates into: "Gee, I didn't really think a black person would be interested in this." The subtext is always, "This is *our* gathering. Be thankful that *we* let you in." It's happened so many times that I know exactly when it's coming. Then they proceed to talk with me about something related *exclusively* to African Americans.

This leads me to my third interactive category—*misguided liberals.* These are the white folks who interact with black folks on a fairly regular basis and constantly pat themselves on the back for their so-called healthy attitudes toward the Great Unwashed. These are some of the ones who staff homeless shelters, or work in soup kitchens, or who attend black churches occasionally. And they work diligently to deliver food and toys during holiday seasons. They bend over backward to ensure that they never say anything that could insult a black person, and when they accidentally (or believe they accidentally) do, they agonize over their mistakes. To cite a brief example: I encountered one of my elderly white male colleagues in the hallway a few years ago after we hadn't seen each other for a while. "God, Trudier," he said, "I haven't seen you in a coon's age." Then he freaked out when he realized what he had said and apologized profusely. Again, I laughed. He felt it necessary to come to my office a couple of days later and apologize some more. I know the expression, but I don't know its origins. In a different setting, another white person with whom I was friendly used the same expression with me and was still apologizing years later. It's just an expression, for goodness sake. One apology is enough.

This kind of example is trivial to me. What matters more is when misguided liberalism has damaging effects. A black female student withdrew from one of my African American literature courses after she earned a grade of C minus on a paper. She e-mailed me immediately after receiving the paper and indicated that she was "very disturbed" and wanted to discuss it with me. When we met, I made it clear that she could rewrite the paper if she wanted to. That was unacceptable to her. The problem was not her but me, because she had never received a C minus on a paper before. She asserted that she had made A minuses on papers submitted to a white professor in her major. I was obviously shocked. Here was a young black woman, who didn't know the function of a comma, who produced numerous run-on sentences throughout her paper, who could not sustain a thesis, and who used *exactly* the same sentence phrasings ten times in a seven-page paper. Whoever told the young lady she wrote at an A minus level was probably a misguided liberal who didn't care what happened to this woman once she left the university; the professor merely wanted to preserve her reputation as a person who wasn't tough on African Americans.

I place these liberals side by side with the folks I call *apologists*. These are the white people who always make excuses for other white people when it looks as if those folks have engaged in racist behavior. So they will say to me about the woman giving out better-than-earned grades: "Well, maybe she thought if she gave her an A minus she would be inspired to learn how to write better." They are the folks who say, "Your colleagues in the English department might just be preoccupied when you encounter them in the hallway." They are the folks who say, "You're overreacting. When folks greet you at parties, they are just being nice." They are the folks who say—when you recount a blatant racist incident to them —"Well, I'm *sure* he didn't mean it that way. You're probably just being a little paranoid."

So, for a moment, why don't we just say that I have a healthy dose of paranoia. After all, I did have one of those signs for years that read: "Just because you're paranoid doesn't mean they're not out to get you." Let's say that I'm paranoid in ten percent of the instances where I believe I encounter racist attitudes. What are you going to do with the other ninety percent? Let's say that I could be paranoid in fifty percent of the cases. What are you going to do with the other fifty percent? As long as there is something that creates a problem, then we *have not* reached the point where acceptance is in the heart rather than in the law.

In 1987 a black male friend of mine died of lupus. He taught in the Department of Communication Studies at the University of North Carolina at Chapel Hill. *Dr.* Wallace Ray Peppers. After his death we established an award in his name. He used to say that he was going to write a book about white people. It would be entitled "The Things They Have Said to Me." He would begin, he said, with a note he received from a graduate student that began, "*Wallace,* Dr. Jamison says you should . . ." That disrespect, he asserted, was the essence of his experience in that department.

I often think of Wallace and how I could complete the book he intended to write. Here are some of the things that have been said to me over the years.

➤ When I taught at another college, I presented that English department with the strongest tenure case it had seen in ten years. The year before, however, four white males had been tenured, and one of them had been approved unanimously. When the vote on my case was counted, there were twenty-one in favor and one against. I was told that there was one vote against me because the person casting the vote knew that his single negative vote *would not* prevent me from getting tenure; he just thought that a white male should retain the status of having the only unanimous tenure vote in that department.

➤ In response to my receiving the highest teaching ratings one year, two of my white male colleagues came to me and said, laughingly, "You'd better stop getting such good teaching ratings, or we're going to break both your legs."

➤ When I was appointed to a special professorship, one of my colleagues' responses was: "Now that you're a chaired professor, what are you gonna do? Buy another big ol' car?" At the time I was driving a Pontiac 6000; I had never thought of that as a big ol' car, yet this person, in her annoyance with my good fortune, could only stereotype me in the "colored person buying Cadillac" mold.

➤ Once when I asked a question in a meeting, one of my white male colleagues responded afterward with, "Trudier, you always go for the balls." For asking a question. I doubt that he would have used the word "balls" with a white woman; I gave him the chance to be risqué.

➤ When I was speaking of some of my research about black subjects, one of my colleagues asked, "Why don't you teach at a historically black college?" The irony is that if I taught at a historic black college, I would probably specialize in Shakespeare or Wordsworth, for in those traditionally black environments, black teachers specialize in *everything;* they are not cordoned off, as they frequently are in predominantly *white* colleges and universities, to teach *only* those things originating from black folks.

It's a wonder we're not all crazy or dead. My major preoccupation in life is managing madness. So, you ask, how do I do that? How do I keep on going on in the face of racism that does not exhibit itself in blatant insults or physical abuse, but in the symbolic "death of a thousand cuts"? Chester B. Himes, in his novel *If He Hollers Let Him Go,* depicts a dream that his protagonist, Bob Jones, has. He dreams of a fight between a black person and a white person, and he can't figure out—for the longest time—what weapon the white person is using. Then he realizes that it's a knife no longer than a razor blade. The man just keeps sticking and sticking at the black man. No one wound, indeed no several wounds, will be fatal, but eventually the accumulation can be The Death of a Thousand Cuts.

I survive in the face of a thousand insults with an abundance of humor and a great family tradition. Zora Neale Hurston, author of *Their Eyes Were Watching God*, talks in one of her books about the value of humor to African American survival. Long before I read Hurston, however, I, like many other black folks, knew that in the face of events you cannot control, you have to find some sanity-saving way of dealing with them. Humor, like the blues, is laughing to keep from crying.

I have also been blessed with a wonderful family, especially my mother. I figure that if my mother worked for fifteen dollars a week to support a family of eight, and if she had to deal with the racist Ku Klux Klansman who owned the grocery store in our neighborhood, then surely I can deal with people who refuse to recognize my existence. So I do what I do because I always remember my family, especially my mother. And I just happen to love what I do.

I realize that racism will not be cured in my lifetime nor in the lifetime of anyone I know. Racist issues will *always* surface. It makes me tired. Still, I encourage those who are hopeful. One fall I taught a seminar entitled "Martin Luther King, Jr.: His Legacy in African American Literature." It was fascinating to see how little my students knew of the civil rights period in America, and it was equally fascinating to note the extent to which they believed they have progressed beyond, and are immune to, race and racism. I did not spend time disabusing them of these notions. They should make their own discoveries. To their credit, they read widely and learned quickly. One way they can continue their learning is through the media.

Two recent movies highlight racial interactions in America. One of them is Spike Lee's *Bamboozled,* the controversial movie about blacks performing in blackface, which excavates an ugly phase of American history, and the other is *The Ladies Man,* a comedy focusing on two stereotypes of black men: their desire for white women and their excessive sexual endowment. Both movies raised a lot of eyebrows. But they make clear that the levels at which blacks and whites in this country are able to perceive and interact with each other will provide troubled interpretations for a long time to come.

I am not glowingly optimistic about race relations in America or in the South. I don't think that I'm excessively pessimistic either. But I do harbor questions about where, if at all, fruitful conversations can begin between blacks and whites in the South. Then I think of my friend Julia. I met her in 1973 when she inquired about auditing a folklore class I was teaching. White, twenty-three years older than I, and divorced by that time, she and her adolescent daughter soon became fixtures in my life. Not only did she audit the course, but we began to share meals, social outings, travel, and a love of books and storytelling. Julia loved Christmas, so much so that she had named her daughter "Holly," collected Christmas books, and set up a Christmas tree one July and exchanged presents with a friend whom she had not seen for many years. Whenever I traveled to interesting sights, I searched for Christmas books for Julia. I enlisted a fellow traveler in one such search in Milan, Italy, and ironically located only a Christmas book that had been published in the United States. The storekeeper was kind enough to inscribe it to Julia in Italian, so at least she had that much of a foreign memento.

Julia and I were certainly aware of race in our relationship, but it never mattered beyond selecting soul food or continental cuisine for our meals until around 1980, when she visited me in Chapel Hill. One of my brothers, his wife, and their young son were also visiting. After hearing all of us address the child as "boy" on several occasions, as in "Boy, get out of those weeds!" and "Boy, leave those books alone!" Julia asked: "Why do you keep calling him 'boy' when you don't want white people to do it when he grows up?" I had given little thought to "boy" in the context of negative racial overtones; it was just an affectionate way of referring to my nephew. Julia's question led to a discussion of how terms get wielded across racial lines. I can't say the conversation led us to quit using the word, but it did lead me to contemplate how black people can at times be knowingly complicitous in keeping racial slurs alive and well. And it led to many discussions that Julia and I have had about race over the years.

In the thirty years I have known her, I have found Julia to be consistently altruistic, racially aware, and without racist connotations to that awareness. Her existence is a constant positive counterpart to the racial insanity I encounter and lets me know that the world is so much larger, freer, and human than the absurdities I have witnessed or heard over the years.

But I am also a realist, albeit a romantic one, and from where I sit, the good folks like Julia have little influence over the individuals and institutions that perpetuate a system of unchanging racism. Yet I recognize that people of African descent in America are a *long* way from where we used to be. We measure progress in inches, not miles, and we can only hope that the Julias of the South—together with their racism-resisting sisters in the tradition of novelist Lillian Smith and social activist Jessie Daniel Ames—will someday inspire all their compatriots to different ways of interacting with and appreciating people on Southern soil who do not share their skin coloring.

CHAPTER SIXTEEN

Nursing Home

When my mother's condition deteriorated to the point that it was necessary for us to move her to a nursing home, we were fortunate to find one a mere six miles from the house in which she had lived for twenty-five years. In the almost six years that she was a resident there, I made visits as frequently as I could. Depending on her condition, my sisters and I alternated spending nights with her. From the moment my mother arrived at the facility, her world and ours was transformed. She had to adjust to a fish-bowl existence, and we had to adjust to the fact that this woman who had been so strong for us for so many years was now in need of our strength. We tried hard, therefore, to make her residency at the home as palatable and as comfortable as it could be under the circumstances. In the process we received the education of our lives.

Nursing homes are, by their nature, holding pens that contain human beings until they die. Alice Walker calls them human zoos. Though I would perhaps stop short of that description, it does come close. During the nearly six years that I went to the nursing home in which my mother resided, there was drama of some kind or another almost every day. Some days it would be the woman down the hall who hollered nonstop. Or the woman across the hall from her who,

Bible on her lap, would endlessly yell "Help me!" in the most unsettling voice. Or it would be the elementary school teacher who long ago had been deposited at the home by someone (we never knew if it was relatives or the state; no one ever came to visit her); desperately she was always looking for some papers to grade. The direct-care workers would calm her down by giving her a pad and pen with which to "take names" of her students.

Some of the most dramatic moments were provided by Veronica Reynolds, the elderly African American wife of a minister. She apparently had been put in the nursing home simply because her equally elderly husband could not take care of her, and they had no children. So she was pissed. And she let the world know it. She sat in the door of her room, which was just down the hall from my mother's room, and minded everybody's business. She would direct other residents about where and how to drive their wheelchairs, how they should wear their clothes, and what they should be doing at any given moment of the day. My sisters and I concluded that her husband had put her in the nursing home to get away from her. When the sheer force of her will did not get other residents to follow her directives, she resorted to profanity. Now *that* was noteworthy—the wife of a minister cursing out people in a nursing home. On one occasion to which I can attest, "V" was in her room. Someone passed her door and yelled out, "Hey, Miss V!" "Who the *hell* is that calling me V?" she yelled back, and the chagrined worker slunk on down the hall.

Miss V specialized in giving everybody hell except the members of my family. She was almost always sitting in her doorway four doors away when I went to visit Miss Unareed, so I assumed that was the case with other of my relatives as well. She would look up when I arrived, call out "Hey, Baby," and something like, "Y'all sho take good care of yo' momma." Her voice was noticeably quieter at these moments. My sister Ann and I developed the habit of calling her Mrs. Reynolds, and she seemed to appreciate that. I believe she was also nice to us because we were what she did not have —offspring to take care of her. We represented a lack in her life, one before which she was at least quieter if not completely humble.

Calling Miss V "Mrs." Reynolds was also important. It was going against the grain of prevailing nursing home practice, and that practice was generally against African American cultural norms. Direct-care workers referred to most of the elderly people in the home by their first names. That was especially conspicuous because most of them were under thirty, while most of the residents were over seventy. It was also conspicuous because almost all the direct-care workers were African American, as was a substantial percentage of the residents. The residents, therefore, were old enough to be grandmothers to most of these young women (these direct-care workers were almost always female). What these young women did in the nursing home every day was thus antithetical to what they had been taught in their black communities. Although it might have given them some sense of power over or equality with the white residents, it made them disrespectful to the black residents.

When the first one of them called my mother by her first name, therefore, Ann set them straight. "My mother," she said, "is old enough to be your grandmother. You may call her Miss Unareed or Mrs. Harris, but you may not call her Unareed." It was interesting to watch how the directive took. My mother was thereafter generally called "Miss Unareed" or

"Mrs. Harris," and many of the young women who worked with her did indeed become comparable to grandchildren. Two or three of them would often gather in her room to take breaks or complete their paperwork, and they would bring their young children to visit her. Miss Unareed would love up on those kids as eagerly as she loved up on my goddaughter's three children or her biological grandchildren and great-grandchildren.

My mother's room was located at the intersection of T-shaped hallways. On bright, sunny days, someone coming up the hall from the bottom of the T could look into her room and out the window to the parking lot, a grassy knoll, and part of the street beyond. Persons whose powers of perception were deteriorating faster than others would sometimes think that my mother's room was the way out of the nursing home. On several occasions they would walk into Momma's room as if they were planning to walk straight on through the window and out into the open. One man was determined that just beyond the window in Momma's room was the barn near his house. He needed to get through and put some tools in his shed before it rained. He made that trip to her room countless times before he was permanently confined to bed.

My mother's room was also a source of attraction because it was stocked with two glass containers and a drawer partially filled with candy. Long before she went to the nursing home, Momma made it a nightly ritual to suck on peppermint candy. Once in the nursing home, and with the consent of her physician, her supply remained constant. Wandering residents and direct-care workers soon learned that Miss Unareed's room was sweet haven, so the candy disappeared unbelievably quickly. First it was peppermint and Tootsie Roll pops.

Momma liked the red ones, so we made it clear to those wandering visitors that they could take any they wanted *except* those. We had relatives in various parts of Tuscaloosa looking for Tootsie Rolls pops and, on more than one occasion, I stocked up in Chapel Hill before making a trip to Alabama. Tootsie Rolls and peppermints gave way to various kinds of mints and other suckable pops.

Miss Unareed could literally take a nap while sucking on one of her pops. They were also a way of calming her down when she became agitated. Either because of medication or the consequences of Alzheimer's, she smacked a couple of nurses and direct-care workers. More often, she would latch onto somebody's hair and not let go while they were changing her or giving her medication (she caught my locks on several occasions). With her supergrip the only way to get her to let go of the hair or the wrist around which her hand was locked was to offer her a lollipop of one kind or another. We were lucky if she took it within a few seconds; sometimes the hard-locked person had to wait for a couple of minutes. She would then take the candy, offer the sweetest smile, and proceed to suck away as if nothing unusual had happened.

Although my mother did occasionally become agitated, her moments of aggravation were minimal in comparison to those of several residents. Some were so vicious that the direct-care workers did not want to work with them. It was an interesting commentary on the kinds of deterioration that occur in elderly people, in body as well as in attitude. Anger and depression seemed to be the dominant responses to the aging process, with anger seeming to be even more prevalent than depression. It was not unusual to see a couple of residents engaging in a cursing match, and I would think, "My goodness, what happens to the socialization process as one grows older?" It seemed as if everything they had learned about being nice to people when they were children or self-sufficient adults was discarded in this environment. They did everything with impunity and seemingly with little consciousness of consequences. One woman down the hall from my mother would move her wheelchair to the door of the room next door. Apparently one of the women there had the habit of taking another woman's clothes out of her closet and moving them into her own (one of the many unconscious things in which people with deteriorated mental capacities engage). The uninvited visitor would sit in the doorway and harass the closet intruder: "Leave her clothes alone. You ain't got no business moving her stuff to your closet. Damn it! I said leave her stuff alone. You keep that up, and I'm going to come in there and whip your ass. Stupid white bitch."

And there was the race issue—smack dab in the middle of an environment where basic human leveling might be thought to eliminate that. Especially not so in this nursing home. Angry black women might curse out other residents and direct-care workers. Angry white women, however, could and did play the traditional race card. White Miss Melton was probably about eighty-six, scooting around the home in a wheelchair. She had to be lifted in and out of bed, in and out of the wheelchair, bathed, dressed, and groomed. There was almost nothing she could do for herself beyond feeding herself. Yet when a black direct-care worker would locate her in the hallway and approach her about getting her bath, Miss Melton would resort to racist slurs that would make any sensitive human being cringe: "You black bitch. Don't put your nigger hands on me. I don't want you damn niggers doing anything for me." And yet her family had left her in the care of the "niggers," for they never came to see her. She would fight and call out insults until she disappeared in the bathroom.

How must it feel to know that you have been abandoned by everybody white, the folks with whom you identify, and that you are being touched and cared for by the "niggers"? Can such behavior be excused on the basis that these are pathetic old people in a nursing home whose social skills have been stripped beyond recovery? I think not. Miss Melton wanted to return to the early days of the twentieth century when it was acceptable for her to feel superior to people of African descent. I wonder what the direct-care workers must feel when they have to clean feces and urine from the body of someone who is calling them "nigger" throughout the process. How must they feel when they know that they are trying to prolong this person's life by preventing breakdown of her skin when she is challenging their very connectedness to her humanity? Do they do their jobs merely because they are the jobs they have been trained to do, no matter the abuse? Or do they do their jobs because they have developed a greater sense of transcendence? Do they say, "She just old, so I'm gon' ignore her"? Or are there genuine moments when they would like to retaliate? Is it reasonable to expect that, day in and day out, they will willingly suffer such abuse without some form of retaliation? I have heard the abuse, but I never heard of any instance in which a direct-care worker was reprimanded for mistreating a patient. It would be easy, however, for such a worker, if she were less sensitive than the ones who worked in this home, simply to let Miss Melton slip in the bathtub and break a hip that could end her life. No one ever did. Their reactions to racist Miss Melton and those like her were another sign that we had put Miss Unareed in the "right" nursing home. With her "thank-yous" and "pleases" and her great smile, she was a hit with most of the direct-care workers.

These workers changed her and fed her when we were not around, gave her baths, and changed her linen. Though they might all have been relatively eager workers, Momma trusted some of them more than others. Instinctively, even when she could not speak, she knew which ones she preferred to have work with her. On one occasion, when a woman who was about five feet tall was working with Ann to change Momma, and the woman offered to hold Momma up while Ann did the changing, Momma said, "Unh um." Ann traded positions with the woman, held Momma up, and saw a big smile spread over Momma's by-now toothless mouth. To Momma, who was about five-feet-eight-inches tall, this rather small person looked more like a child and she was not comfortable with this "child" trying to hold her up.

The workers were generally helpful, supportive, and responsive, and there were many of them over the years, because nursing homes are notorious for their hard work, poor pay, and high turnover rates. Of the many direct-care personnel who worked with Momma during her residency, there were a few laggards whom we were not unhappy to see leave, but there were only two whose departures we applauded; one requested a transfer from working with my mother because she felt she was getting too old (she had been working at the home for twenty-five years) to do the kind of lifting that was required with my mother. The other felt that she could not meet Ann's standards for how Momma should be treated. Both of these reasons were acceptable severances as far as I was concerned.

One thing we learned early about even so-called good nursing homes: there is a hierarchy of care. Residents whose relatives are vigilant receive a bit more than regular attention, which means that their soiled clothing might actually be changed at the stipulated two-hour intervals. Those not so fortunate might lie in their own urine and feces for hours. As a mostly mobile patient whom we would not allow to be confined permanently to bed even after her second hip replacement operation, my mother received special attention in addition to that provided by the nursing home staff. The sitters we hired, with a couple of exceptions, took very good supplemental care of my mother. One of the exceptions, a young woman, had come to us and asked if she could have the job. We were to discover why she was so eager. She viewed working for my mother as the opportunity to study for her college courses. Because my mother's speech was deteriorating in 1998, she could not gather the words to tell us what was happening. It became clear, though, one day when Ann did her customary close examination of Momma's thighs and hips. There were the telltale little red spots of early skin breakdown. The woman had been allowing Momma to sit in her urine for longer periods than was acceptable. Because we caught the spots early, we could treat them easily. Firing the offender was barely sufficient, I thought, for her threatening my mother's physical health and for the fraud she had tried to perpetrate on my family.

The other woman we hired was even slicker. By 2000, when this woman worked the 6:00–11:00 P.M. shift, Momma was mostly silent and usually ready for a nap by this time of day (Alzheimer's had pretty much taken her speech). So our offending sitter would come directly from her other job and use part of the time with my mother to sleep. The longer she worked for us, the more lax she apparently became. She didn't try to engage Momma, or keep her alert, or carry out any of her other specified interactive duties. She checked her periodically for wetness and elimination, and she slept in between. We heard rumors but we were not able to confirm them for ourselves until, on a trip home to Alabama, I went to the nursing home one evening around 6:30 P.M. and found the woman sound asleep. We fired her as well. People can be devastated by disease alone; but if someone is going to share the same physical space with them, ostensibly as a helper, then the victim ought at least to know that that so-called helper is present. Also, this second attempt to defraud my family, like the first one, was so insulting to the memory of my mother's honesty and sense of fair play—not to mention her health—that I felt absolutely no remorse at all for what I considered a justified termination.

Other drama at the nursing home was provided by volunteers, white and black, who came in to cheer up the residents in some way, those proverbial do-gooders who believe that a two-hour stint in a nursing home twice a year takes care of their charity. These intrusions were at least rare. The regular do-gooders were the royal pains. They would come faithfully, on whatever day of the week their church or community organization had chosen, and try their best to stimulate some response from the residents. The most enthusiastic of these were the singers. Some came with guitars and moved from room to room standing in the doorways and singing for people who mainly ignored them. At times, I'm sure the response to their singing must have been worse than that received by telemarketers. However, that never deterred any of these folks. Rejects from choirs or failures at club auditions ended up singing to people in nursing homes. It gave new definition to the meaning of "captive audience," and it must have expanded the definition of ego. Whether standing in the residents' doorways with guitars in hand, or playing piano for and singing to residents who had been collected and delivered to a common space, these wannabe stars were as enthusiastic as if they were performing at Carnegie Hall. Sometimes a few of the residents tried to sing along, or waved their hands and heads to the music, patted their feet, or clapped their hands. Most of them, however, just retained the alpha stares that defined them as being in worlds beyond the reach of music. Early in her residence at the home, Miss Unareed didn't mind being wheeled to the common room to listen to some of these folks; then she started talking through the singing, and she finally ended up, as many of her equally hard-of-hearing compatriots did, simply sleeping through the antics. The lack of interest of some audience members, however, never deterred the performers. It was (and is) a fascinating dynamic in the interplay of charity and aging.

For all this constant stimulation around the nursing home, forced and otherwise, the time came when Momma moved further into a world of silence, when she could no longer string together words and sentences. Even after she could no longer articulate her desires, wants, needs, wishes, or anything else to us, however, she retained her smile, the alertness and brightness in her eyes, and her desire to hug. She would also reach out and touch our arms or whatever parts of our bodies she could reach, or hold our hands. So we continued to communicate in those ways that mothers and children have despite obstacles. When we fed her some of the specially prepared pureed food that had no resemblance or taste to anything we could name, if she didn't like it, she would spit it out. Some folks might call that gross; I call it communication

(Ann would then make her some special pureed treat, such as peaches, cantaloupe, watermelon, or baked sweet potatoes). When she wanted to "tell on" someone in the nursing home, she would point toward them, wink at us, and burst into laughter. She gave the lie to anyone who asserts that people with Alzheimer's cannot learn new things, for her winking was definitely something new. She expressed other things to us by grunts, hugs, or smiles. I think she and Ann had a special spiritual connection, because Ann almost always knew exactly what she wanted.

Within the nursing home and to regular visitors, my mother was known for her appearance. First, her hair. It was always shampooed, cut, curled, and permed—none of those weeklong hairstyles that many women in nursing homes are left to endure. Never did Ann allow Momma's hair to look raggy just because she was in a nursing home. The same was true of her clothes. She had closet upon closet full of clothing (transferred from home according to the seasons) and was changed into clean outfits as often as three and four times a day. The trick we learned in the first couple of years was to buy one or two tops and three or four skirts or pairs of pants, since bottoms were prone to getting soiled faster than tops. Not once did we allow the laundry staff at the home to wash her clothes. "Yo' mama got some really nice clothes," one of the direct-care workers told Ann within a week of Momma's arrival at the home. "I wouldn't put them in the laundry if I were you. They mix up colors and cause things to fade on each other, and they *always* lose stuff." So for those almost six years, Ann, with occasional help from relatives and neighbors, washed everything my mother wore. She even washed the nursing home diapers that Momma used and that were labeled with her name and room number. I have joined in washing and drying as many as six heavy duty loads of clothing in a weekend, so this commitment was a major one. (We had just bought a new washer and dryer less than three weeks before Momma died.)

Miss Unareed's beautiful—and always beautifully clean—outfits were accessorized with earrings and breast pins and, early on, makeup and sometimes a bracelet or rings. Her outfits were topped off with the cologne my brother Husain provided from his store, Husain's Fashions, to go along with the earrings and pins he donated. He also regularly contributed new clothing, as did other family members. Ann shopped for the rest and became known as one of the expert locators of sales in Tuscaloosa and the surrounding areas. Momma was therefore always dressed to the nines, sweet smelling, and perfectly coifed. Several folks thought that we kept her dressed so well because we were keeping up her identity as a former schoolteacher. They were surprised to learn that this woman who won nursing home beauty contests had been the wife of a cotton farmer and had also worked as a domestic, a janitor, and a cook. Their stereotypes of how teachers might dress were emphatically short-circuited when I, the schoolteacher daughter, showed up in comfortable tops, pants, and running shoes. Miss Unareed, I maintain, could outdress me any day. For that reason I referred to her at times as "the beauty queen" or "the queen." I like to think that, despite her ever failing mental and motor capacities, despite her retreat into silence, despite her moving backward into a childhood that encouraged *us* to mother *her*, we treated her like a queen every day.

Certainly nursing homes can be depressing places, and certainly during my mother's stay in this one I saw some depressing things, but I also believe that environments can be changed—if only in small ways. So we had prominent decorations in Momma's room, including a sketch of several church-lady types who were fishing from a bridge. We also had flowers, photographs of family members, and several other personal items. Ann changed the decorations as the seasons changed, even incorporating secular holidays such as Halloween. On each April 26, we celebrated Miss Unareed's birthday with a party at the home, to which, in addition to family members, many of the residents invited themselves. The full course home-cooked meals were an obvious attraction, as were the balloons, streamers, and table decorations. I am delighted that I took time to go home to Alabama for each of those birthdays.

We survived the nursing home with imagination and patience. Miss Unareed, as we knew from the beginning, would not survive it. Yet we came to know that space because of her, and many of the residents, their families, and the direct-care workers are still in our lives. The sitters who were working with Momma in 2001 regularly ask about family members and check on our status. In some ways it might be said that we gave up one family member, indeed our most important family member, in exchange for her very rich legacy. That legacy includes a host of renewed family bonds and many new relationships. Our family came together and stuck together in impressive ways during those almost six years, and many of the people we met will remain in our lives. Although none of this can replace Miss Unareed, it signals to me again and again that nursing home experiences, while never a desirable substitute for living in one's own space, do not ultimately have to be the utterly horrible experiences they are frequently portrayed as being.

CHAPTER SEVENTEEN

Summer Snow

IT HAS TAKEN me a long time to arrive at a basic fact of my existence: I am a Southerner. For a black person to claim the South, to assert kinship with the territory and the mores that most black folks try to escape, is about as rare as snow falling in Tuscaloosa during dog days. It's a reconciliation that many African Americans have not yet made. Of course millions of black people *live* in the South, but I think they—and I among them for the longest time—view themselves as separate from whatever aura the South exudes as a political, social, regional entity. It's almost as if there are nations within nations in the South, and African Americans form one of those nations. Historically, we had to deal with whites, we understood what it meant for them to consider themselves Southern, and we didn't want to be a part of it. We could be from Alabama or Georgia or Mississippi and act as if that space were somehow psychologically removed from the geographical region of the country that retained the bloodiest history and the most negative race relations.

So why, all of a sudden, am I a "Southerner" instead of "living in the South," and what does that designation mean? Let me first explain what it does *not* mean. It certainly doesn't mean that I approve of racism or of the Confederate flag flying over the capitol in South Carolina or other Southern states. I do not now, nor have I ever, embraced the Confederate flag. To illustrate the point: In 2000, Charles H. Rowell, editor of *Callaloo,* invited me to contribute to a special issue devoted to discussions of the Confederate flag. A contribution could have been essay, memoir, or creative. My schedule did not allow me to complete the assignment, but I did have a contribution in mind. It would focus on a poor black woman in some isolated part of the South who would go into the local Klan-owned grocery/retail store and ask for the Confederate flags the management had advertised as give-aways. Every time a new batch comes into the store, she is the first there to request a few, sometimes going away with four or five at a time. Local whites are curious about this, and blacks who hear about it are stupefied. The woman is always grateful for the flags, but she never offers an explanation as to why she wants them. She doesn't have a flagpole from which to fly a single one of her many flags. Finally, the narrator follows the woman home and finds her in the backyard, with a roaring fire going around a cast-iron pot in which she has placed her new batch of flags. She is stirring them with a long wooden "bleaching spoon," and the narrator describes the red, white, and blue giving way to snowy white. The woman bleaches and rinses, bleaches and rinses, then hangs the now all-white cloth on the outdoor lines to dry. When the sun has dried them thoroughly, she takes them down, carefully tears them into strips about fifteen inches wide, and places them in the bulging drawer of rags that she uses for sanitary napkins.

Ah, but would such a tale gross people out? Would it seem too bitter? Too cute? Could the material from which flags are made ever be so bleachable into whiteness, or so pliable as to be used in such intimate connection with the human body? I don't know. I do know that contemplation of that symbol has to be as much on an emotional level as on an intellectual one. That is the only way I can respond to it, and I'm sure that's the response of many black Southerners. So claiming "Southernness" doesn't mean I'm ready to go wave Confederate flags or participate in reenactments of the Civil War.

Being a Southerner *definitely* doesn't mean that I like the idea of a secessionist teaching at my undergraduate alma mater. I was shocked in 2000 when a friend of mine at Duke University called me up to ask if I had seen a newspaper article about my undergraduate school. It focused on one of the key figures in a movement to reconstitute the pre–Civil War South. This man, a historian, was quietly going about the business of teaching at my little school in Tuscaloosa. In his off time, however, he was apparently distributing key information to other white men who felt as he did. Why, I asked myself, if he believed so fervently in his cause, did he teach at a historic black college? There was an incongruity there that I have not yet resolved. And my school hasn't either. The negative publicity may have died down, but the spotlight certainly didn't help the school, and those of us who are graduates remain puzzled as to how he came to be on the faculty in the first place.

And being a Southerner cannot possibly mean that I like the way our educational systems, after all these years, still favor non–African American children. I mentor a high school student in Chapel Hill. On one occasion when she was in elementary school, she made a B in math, although she had A's in all of her other subjects. When her parents and I questioned the teacher about the grade, she assured us that it was "a very good grade." But, we said, there's the whole range of A beyond that. The teacher was literally surprised that we found the B grade problematic, which signaled to my mind that the B range was the highest that teacher expected of the student, or the highest grade she was willing to give this particular black student.

In another instance, when my mentee was in the sixth grade, I had a conference with her core teachers. She had done very well for an extended period, and then all of a sudden, there was a dramatic drop in her grades. Well, it turned out that she had been hanging out with a group of black girls whom the teachers judged to be problematic. The thing that was most striking about this conversation was that all the core teachers realized that my mentee could make A's. They had concluded, however, that the black girls with whom she hung out could not; indeed, they could not be counted on to make C's or D's. Thus, at the ages of eleven and twelve, these four or five little black girls had been dismissed as not worth worrying about as far as these white teachers were concerned, because the paths that they had obviously carved out for themselves were not going to be ones that led to college and professions. Instead, these teachers were convinced, the girls' paths would lead to babies out of wedlock or jobs at McDonald's. So they had already dismissed these children. They had lowered their expectations to the point of no return. I am confident that when the children sensed that in their teachers, they lived *down* to those expectations by acting out, making frequent trips out of class, and otherwise being problematic. Their bodies were present, but their minds were *long gone* from the experience of education. A South whose teachers produce these kinds of mental vacations is not the one I am embracing when I confess to being a Southerner.

So what does my new status mean? It means, first of all, that I am most comfortable living east of the Mississippi and south of Washington, D.C., perhaps because I like "town"

America more than "city" America. It means that I have come to identify with and—dare I say it?—defend this region of the country as a viable and pleasant place to live. My Southernness, like my Americanness, has been bored into my bones in part as a result of reading, teaching, traveling, and perusing the media. When I am north of the Mason-Dixon line and some smug person dares to start downing my home state of Alabama—without ever having set foot in the state, indeed without having set foot outside of New England—that annoys me, and I feel compelled to offer an alternative to his or her stereotyped evaluations.

The smugness with which some black Northerners assert that they have no enslaved persons in their family history is absolutely infuriating. That assertion, they believe, exempts them from a shared history of violence, exploitation, and exclusion with blacks who do have slavery as a part of their history. The South is anathema to these Northerners, and they feel so smugly justified in heaping derision upon it as well as upon those of us who are presumably stupid enough to live here and claim that history. These folks would never consider attending colleges or universities in the South or sending their kids to them. Vacationing in Mobile would be like volunteering to go to hell. These are the folks who, as playwright Alice Childress would say, wear my soul case thin.

Do they really think we believe all the hype about the North? Do they really think that Roxbury is the same as Beacon Hill, or that the South Side of Chicago is the same as Michigan Avenue, or that Harlem evokes the same financial response as Wall Street? Or that Roxbury, the South Side, and Harlem are infinitely superior to Atlanta, Memphis, New Orleans, and several other places in the South? It seems to me that a lot of these folks are quick to put down the South because they are insecure about their own positions in the North. If things are so wonderful everywhere up there, then why the need to pick on us at all? I believe it happens in part because the South is still fair game, the one part of the country that, because of its history, few people feel as if they will meet with any opposition if they pick on it. So their statements "How can you stand it down there?" and "I wouldn't live down there for anything in the world" really boil down to that age-old human tendency to feel superior to somebody or something.

When I am in Spain or Jamaica and some smug person dares to commiserate with me because, to her or him, I live in such an abominable part of the United States, that annoys me, and I feel compelled to reject that sympathy. Perhaps it is because their countries are older, or they too fall into the bid for superiority, but it is nonetheless annoying. When foreigners most often arrive on United States soil, they head for the big cities, like New York and San Francisco. It might take them a while to get to a Southern city like Atlanta—if they get there at all—so it is easy for them to read or watch a few things and generalize about the South. For those foreigners who want to assimilate into American culture as quickly as they can, they "do as the Romans do" in maligning the South. I would much prefer to offer them a guided tour of Southern territory than to suffer their romanticized sympathy in Madrid or Montego Bay. The South is not paradise, but it's not the devil's home base either.

There is, as the late Margaret Walker asserts in her poem "October Journey," a beauty and an ugliness about our Southern homes. She, among all the African American writers of her generation, moved south (in the 1940s after schooling in the North) and stayed south. For more than fifty years, she wrote from Jackson, Mississippi, with a penetrating, unromanticized eye about this "cultured hell" of a region. Walker was ahead of her time in staking her claim in the South; after all, it became fashionable to return to the region only in the 1970s.

For me to deny the South is to deny all the people who made me who and what I am. Despite the racist environment in which he lived and worked in Alabama, my father was nonetheless able to buy a farm and to support his family. He held on to that property until his death. By his example he instilled in his children the value of owning one's own space in the world and, where possible, one's own business. This man who had two years of formal schooling was able to live and thrive in an environment in which very well-educated black Northerners, by their avowed preconceptions, would not be able to survive.

Despite having attended segregated schools, I was nonetheless able to compete effectively enough to be awarded fellowships to earn graduate degrees. When I arrived at The Ohio State University, I learned that I was just as prepared as any other student to pursue doctoral work. Indeed, during my first summer session there in 1969, I made two A's when college teachers who were returning for work on advanced degrees, and who were considerably senior to me in education and experience, did not do as well. Although I have not yet learned to speak Spanish or play the piano, two extracurricular objectives I have set for myself, I have managed fairly well in other arenas of mind work. My Southern background has not proven to be a deficiency or a handicap.

Despite George Wallace having been twice elected governor of Alabama, I can still say, emphatically, that Alabama is my home. His presence there did not erase the presence of my ancestors, and the air was not poisoned because he breathed in the same spaces as the people from whom I sprang. Indeed, those folks taught me a lesson about Wallace. When I would call home from graduate school distressed because the people in Alabama had voted, yet again, for George Wallace, they did not in any way see this as a thoroughly negative development. After all, Wallace had done quite a bit for the state. And they had all forgiven him for his racism once he had been shot and confined to a wheelchair. I don't propose to understand the relationship of black folks to George Wallace any more than I propose to understand the relationship of black folks in North Carolina to Jesse Helms, but I do know that they do not consider either one to be the devil incarnate.

The South, I have come to understand, was an especially good training ground in my formative years. If I could survive in a place that did not have my best interests at heart, that indeed was hostile to me, then I could develop coping strategies that would enable me to survive anywhere in the world. It has taken me years to become reconciled to the conditions under which I received that invaluable education. As a friend of mine asserts questioningly, "Once we claim hostile America, can claiming the South be far behind?"

James Baldwin maintained of his problematic relationship to America that he could criticize it because he loved it. And through a series of fictional and nonfictional works, that is precisely what he did. Likewise, having been born and bred in the South, I reserve the right to evaluate it, criticize it, and encourage it always to be the best that it can be. In some small way it's sort of like investing in the stock market. You know it can go crazy on you (as the market did in 2000, 2001, and 2002), or even destroy you, but you just keep thinking that if you nurture it enough, tinker with it enough, the results, one day, will be absolutely stunning.

Acknowledgments

ANY PROJECT COMES TO FRUITION only with the assistance of many persons. I thank my family, first and foremost, just for being themselves.

I give special thanks to Anna H. McCarthy, Lovalerie King, and Wanda C. Morgan for reading the manuscript and offering suggestions and challenges for its improvement.

As usual, I thank the Wintergreen Women Writers, those intense listeners and spiritual encouragers who provide more light in a few days than some folks do in years: Joanne V. Gabbin, Sandra Y. Govan, Daryl Cumber Dance, Karla F. C. Holloway, Joyce Pettis, Opal Moore, Lovalerie King, Ethel Smith, Janus Adams, Toi Derricotte, Eugenia Collier, Nikki Giovanni, Carmen Gillespie, Helen Houston, Pinkie Gordon Lane, Marilyn Mobley McKenzie, Deborah E. McDowell, Jessea Gabbin, Hermine Pinson, Val Gray Ward, Virginia Fowler, Daryl Lynn Dance, Sonia Sanchez, Jacqueline Brice-Finch, Linda Nelson, Paule Marshall, and Maryemma Graham.

I thank Dwight McBride for discussing cotton picking with me, and Debbie Meyer for encouraging me to write in this vein. I thank the sorors of Zeta Phi Beta Sorority, Inc., who have listened to me talk about this collection. Now, ladies, you have the opportunity to read it.